Divingin
Malaysia

DR KURT SVRCULA

Times Editions
Marshall Cavendish

© 2004 Marshall Cavendish International (Asia) Private Limited

Editor: Katharine Brown-Carpenter
Designer: Jailani Basari

Published by **Times Editions**—Marshall Cavendish
An imprint of Marshall Cavendish International (Asia) Private Limited
A member of Times Publishing Limited
Times Centre, 1 New Industrial Road, Singapore 536196
Tel: (65) 6213 9288   Fax: (65) 6285 4871
E-mail: te@sg.marshallcavendish.com
Online Bookstore: www.marshallcavendish.com/genref

Malaysian Office:
Federal Publications Sdn Berhad (General & Reference) (3024-D)
Times Subang
Lot 46, Persiaran Teknologi Subang
Subang Hi-Tech Industrial Park
Batu Tiga, 40000 Shah Alam
Selangor Darul Ehsan, Malaysia
Tel: (603) 5635 2191   Fax: (603) 5635 2706
E-mail: cchong@tpl.com.my

National Library Board Singapore Cataloguing in Publication Data
Svrcula, Kurt.
Diving in Malaysia / Kurt Svrcula.—Singapore : Times Editions, c2004.
p.cm.
ISBN : 981-232-755-X

1. Skin diving—Malaysia—Guidebooks.
2. Scuba diving—Malaysia—Guidebooks I. Title

GV838.673
797.2309595—dc21   SLS2004025733

Printed and bound in Singapore

All photographs by Dr Kurt Svrcula with the exception of the following:
Jason Isley of Scubazoo: 220, 230 (top)

Maps courtesy of the Malaysian Centre for Remote Sensing (MACRES)

Malaysian Centre for Remote Sensing
Ministry of Science, Technology and the Environment

CONTENTS

PREAMBLE

Writing a book about diving in Malaysia is a daunting task. The thousands of kilometres of coastline, hundreds of islands and submerged reefs with their unique and awe-inspiring ecosystems will challenge even the most prolific of authors. Although I do not claim to be an authority on all the dive locations and corresponding marine science subjects, I hope my passion and respect are reflected throughout the book.

I do not profess *Diving in Malaysia* to be an all-encompassing guide to all the dive sites in Malaysia. It is simply not possible to dive the length and breadth of the country's 4800 kilometres of coastline and off the shores of more than 200 islands. In addition, having lived in Malaysia and dived its shores and reefs extensively over the past 20 years, I could not help but become protective of the country that I very much consider my home and its fragile ecosystem. For this reason, as well as making a conscious effort to create awareness of the uniqueness, preservation and sustainable use of Malaysia's natural assets, I have excluded certain destinations. Nevertheless, I believe the destinations and locations included—some old and familiar, others new and exciting—represent the best of what Malaysia's marine ecosystem has to offer.

I have been asked many times which is the best dive destination in Malaysia. Obviously, there is no clear-cut answer as everyone has differing perceptions and expectations. For those with an affinity for pelagic species and deeper dives in crystal clear waters, Layang-Layang Atoll and Pulau Sipadan are probably the choice locations. For 'muck divers' with an infinite amount of patience, the shallows of the reefs around Pulau Mabul, Pulau Kapalai and Pulau Lankayan are preferred. Although perhaps not as breathtaking as exotic Pulau Sipadan, there are many additional locations off the east and west coasts of the peninsula and the numerous surrounding islands, such as Pulau Redang, Pulau Tenggol and Pulau Lang Tengah, that are equally rich in biodiversity.

In recent years, much concern has been raised over the exploitation and lack of care of Malaysia's terrestrial and marine ecosystems. Taking an honest look at the state of our islands and reefs, I would have to admit certain shortcomings are evident, which, if not addressed, will ultimately lead to the destruction of these ecosystems, not only ecologically but also economically. Legislation and regulations have been put in place which threaten to punish those who offend. The perpetual shortage of resources, human or otherwise, however, means these laws cannot usually be enforced. As a result and all too often, we witness thoughtless and careless pollution and wanton destruction of the environment.

I firmly believe that in order to bring about change we have to educate. As the current custodians of the planet, we have an obligation to ensure that the next generation and countless more thereafter inherit a world in balance. While each and every one of us can make a difference through action, educating and creating awareness among the young and instilling a deep appreciation of the natural wonders of the world are the most promising and effective ways forward.

So dive, explore, learn, cherish and respect the magnificent marine treasures of Malaysia. I am convinced that you will come back for more!

ACKNOWLEDGEMENTS

This is not an 'Oscar' litany of every conceivable person who has supported me with this project. However, without the support, contributions and critique of many individuals, this undertaking would have come to nothing. My special thanks and appreciation go to:

Eddy Khi and the staff of Nikon Malaysia who patiently entertained my numerous requests for information and equipment

AirAsia for flying me and my always excess luggage and equipment to all corners of Malaysia

Fuji Malaysia, which generously helped with the films

Redang Bay for hosting me, and Tae Peng for showing me the underwater wonders of Pulau Redang

Clement for dragging me along to Pulau Tenggol although I paid dearly for it by being ravaged by sandflies

The hospitable and helpful staff of Mataking Reef Dive Resort

Kenneth Chung of PSR, who not only was a gracious host in Pulau Lankayan but is also doing an exceptional and important job with Sugud Islands Marine Conservation Area (SIMCA)

Lennard and Alex of Sipadan Water Village Resort for sharing so much of their knowledge on Pulau Sipadan and Pulau Mabul

Lawrence Lee of Layang-Layang

Jennifer and Hock for patiently showing me the magnificent waters of Tunku Abdul Rahman Marine Park

All my friends at Scubazoo in KK, to whom I am truly grateful for advice and support

Kenneth and Raymond, way to go!

Mr Voon of Tropical Dives for helping explore the beauty of Miri's reefs

My buddies Ann, Jet and Richard, patient accomplices

Kay Lee and Mary of the *Kaleebso*

Dr E. Campell for graciously allowing me to use his dive medicine material

Prof Dr Ho Sinn Chye, Director of the Oceanographic Institute, Ministry of

Science and Technology, and Prof Dr Phang Siew Moi of University Malaya

Dato Nik N. Mahmood and Dr Laili of the Malaysian Centre for Remote Sensing (MACRES)

Times Editions—Marshall Cavendish for believing in and backing this project

My wife Suzianna and sons Nikolai and Mikhail, long suffering but always supportive when I go off chasing my dreams

Photography

All underwater pictures were taken with a Nikon F5 AE Titanium housed in a SEACAM housing equipped with an S45 swivel finder. Ports used were a fisheye port and 60mm and 105mm macro ports. Lenses were Nikon AF 16mm 2.8 fisheye, 20mm AF 2.8, 60mm AF 2.8 macro and 105mm AF macro lens. Substrobes used were Ikelite 200 and Nikon SB 28 in a SEACAM system flash housing.

Surface pictures were taken with a NIKON F5 and Nikon D1H and D2H digital SLRs, using 16mm, 20mm, 12–24mm, 24–85mm, 85mm and 70–200 Nikon lenses.

Film stock exclusively used was Fuji Velvia 50 ASA for macro shots and Fuji Provia 100 ASA for wide-angle and topside pictures.

IKONOS and LANDSAT Satellite Image Maps

All maps in this book were kindly provided by the Malaysian Centre for Remote Sensing (MACRES).

INTRODUCTION

Malaysia is richly endowed with everything a visitor might want to experience: friendly, hospitable and peaceful people from diverse cultural and ethnic backgrounds, a modern infrastructure, an astonishing variety of food to satisfy the most adventurous and discerning palate, a sub-tropical climate and an ecosystem that is unique in its richness and diversity.

Malaysia is situated just north of the equator in central Southeast Asia. It is made up of Peninsular Malaysia and Sabah and Sarawak. Peninsular Malaysia is bordered by Thailand in the north while Singapore lies at its southern tip. The states of Sabah and Sarawak are located on the north and northwest coasts of the island of Borneo in the South China Sea, with the Kalimantan region of Indonesia to the south. Peninsular Malaysia has forested mountain ranges running north to south and low-lying coastal plains. The coastline extends 1900 kilometres. The west coast consists of mangrove swamps and mudflats which separate into bays and inlets. The plains in the western part of the peninsula have been cleared and cultivated, while the unsheltered east coast consists of tranquil beaches backed by dense jungle. Sarawak has alluvial and, in places, swampy coastal plains with rivers penetrating the jungle-covered hills and mountains of the interior. Sabah has a narrow coastal plain which gives way to mountains and jungle. Mount Kinabalu, at 4101 metres, is the highest peak in Malaysia. The major islands are Langkawi (a group of 99 islands), Penang and Pangkor off the west coast, and Pulau Tioman, Pulau Redang, Pulau Kapas, Pulau Perhentian and Pulau Rawa off the east coast.

Historically an agricultural and commodity-based economy, Malaysia has become a nation admired among other developing countries for its phenomenal growth, modernisation programs, political stability and abundant natural resources. Under the stewardship of former prime minister Tun Dr Mahatir Mohamed, Malaysia became one of the fastest growing economies in Asia. Massive infrastructure development projects including the North-South Expressway, power generating plants and telecommunication networks, a nationwide network of modern airports as well as the famed Formula 1 circuit Sepang, the Petronas Twin Towers, advanced health care centres and the new administrative centre of Putrajaya have transformed Malaysia into a modern society.

With its free-enterprise economy, Malaysia is among the world's largest producers and exporters of rubber, palm oil, petroleum, timber and pepper. The country has successfully diversified into manufactured goods and major exports include electronic components and equipment, electrical goods, chemicals and textiles. Manufacturing is now Malaysia's largest foreign exchange earner. Tourism is another important pillar of the economy and is the second largest revenue earner for the country.

According to the World Wide Fund for Nature (WWF), Malaysia is home to one of the world's most diverse and all-encompassing ecosystems in the world. It is said to have the marine region with the highest biodiversity in the Indo-Pacific Basin, the oldest rainforest (inhabited by a large number of unique animal species and flora), pristine mangroves, wetlands, river systems, magical islands, hills, mountain ranges and caves.

In recent years, environmentally friendly tourism, or ecotourism, has become popular. Ecotourism includes activities such as trekking, diving, rafting and wildlife observation and, in many instances, is the potential salvation of some of the world's most endangered species and ecosystems. This recent proliferation of ecotourism in Malaysia, primarily generated by foreign visitors (who themselves have often depleted their own nation's natural assets), has given rise to the development of many eco destinations throughout the country.

With its pristine, unspoilt beaches and breathtaking reefs, Malaysia is fast becoming one of the leading dive destinations in the world. It boasts a coastline of 4800 kilometres and over 200 islands including renowned locations such as Pulau Sipadan, Pulau Mabul, Pulau Redang and Layang-Layang Atoll that are visited annually by thousands of divers, naturalists and photographers from around the world.

DIVING IN MALAYSIA

Diving in Malaysia is certainly not a new activity. The pioneers of recreational diving are quick to tell tales of adventure dive trips 20 to 25 years ago to the then obscure and rarely visited islands of Pulau Redang, Pulau Tenggol, Pulau Aur or even Pulau Sipadan. Local folklore has it that camping on the beach, bringing along boat loads of tanks or compressors, food and other essentials, was the order of the day. Most of the divers were locals or expatriates working in Singapore, Malaysia and Brunei, who took the opportunity to get away from buzzing city life to explore the pristine and stupendously rich marine environment of Malaysia's seas.

This all changed with Jacques Cousteau's *Ghost of the Sea Turtles* in 1989. This film documented the breathtaking beauty of Pulau Sipadan, considered by many to be one of the best dive destinations in the world. Overnight, Pulau Sipadan, and by extension Malaysia, proliferated itself as the destination of choice for many overseas divers on the lookout for new discoveries or tired of traditional but overcrowded and over-dived destinations like the Red Sea, the Caribbean and the Maldives. Commercially savvy entrepreneurs and developers were quick to catch on to the potential tourism could bring, and resorts and dive centres started to be developed up and down the east coast of the Malaysian peninsula.

Diving in Malaysia has now become a significant revenue earner for many of the islands on the east coast of the peninsula and Sabah. Apart from the locations themselves, other contributing factors that have helped Malaysia become so attractive are dynamic Malaysian companies marketing Malaysia internationally, a comprehensive and modern transportation and communication infrastructure, reliable domestic and international flights and the largely professionally managed dive centres and resorts.

Peninsular Malaysia has two distinct seasons for divers: March to October and November to February. The former is eagerly awaited by the dive community while the latter is the off season, which is not as popular as only the less attractive west coast locations and the rather more expensive destinations in Sabah, i.e. Pulau Sipadan, Pulau Mabul and Layang-Layang Atoll, are accessible. The further off-shore destinations such as Pulau Tenggol, Pulau Aur and Pulau Dayang experience extremely clear waters and excellent visibility early in the season (March and April) and in September and October.

Today, the most dynamic and fastest-growing island destinations on the east coast of the peninsula are Pulau Redang, Pulau Perhentian and Pulau Tioman whereas Pulau Tenggol and Pulau Lang Tengah have as yet untapped potential. Destinations such as Pulau Kapas, Pulau Gemia, Pulau Aur and Pulau Dayang are geared only for weekend dives, primarily for organised dive groups. Pulau Sipadan, Layang-Layang Atoll, Pulau Mabul, Pulau Kapalai and Pulau Lankayan in Sabah are the most developed destinations and the most professionally managed due to the type and level of diving offered and their international clientele.

Dive trips organised by dive shops in Kuala Lumpur and surrounding areas usually require divers to make their own way to the point of departure. Transfers from the mainland to islands such as Pulau Tioman, Pulau Redang and Pulau Perhentian usually depart early in the morning. The ferries are normally operated by the resorts.

Regular weekend dive trips, either for open water certification or leisure dives, are organised to the east coast from March to October and to Pulau Jarak on the west coast during the northeast monsoon (November to February). Trips to the more exotic locations in Sabah are all-year-round affairs and need to be booked direct with the resort or sales agent. Dive centres also organise group tours to these destinations.

A typical resort or island dive centre set-up is staffed by experienced local instructors and dive masters who have in-depth knowledge of the area's dive sites, highlights and, of course, hazards, be they currents or nasty inhabitants such as the sometimes aggressive titan triggerfish. If knowledge of the local night scene or the best eating places is what you seek, the 'local' boys will be able to point you in the right direction.

Every dive centre offers training and certification from basic to dive master level and is equipped to varying degrees with tanks and rental equipment. The majority of dive centres offer Professional Association of Diving Instructors (PADI) certification but National Association of Underwater Instructors (NAUI), Scuba Schools International (SSI) and British Sub Aqua Club (BSAC) certifications can also be obtained. A comprehensive range of other dive courses conducted by resident instructors can also be taken. However, it is prudent to ensure, among others, that tanks are properly maintained and carry the annual inspection decal (i.e. they have undergone the hydrostatic test for corrosion), oxygen and first-aid facilities are adequate, boat operators are qualified to operate dive boats, good diving practices are observed and care for the environment is shown. If you forget to take along your certification card, a short check-out dive with a dive master is a must.

Typically, 3 to 4 dives per day, including night dives, are offered. The transfer to dive sites at the more frequented destinations is by fibreglass mono-hull, single-engine boats, which can hold 10 to 12 divers. Old, traditional wooden fishing boats also serve as dive boats and have space for 15 or more divers. Most of the boats carry first-aid kits and oxygen for emergencies but it is advisable to check prior to departure. Normally, large buckets of fresh water are available on board for divers to have a quick wash or rinse underwater cameras. It is important to note that dive flags are rarely used and boats are seldom marked as dive boats.

In most cases, descent to the dive sites is free, without the aid of a buoy or shot line unless strong surface currents are present. Some often frequented sites around Pulau Tioman and Pulau Aur have anchor buoys to aid divers to the site but be careful when holding onto the line as microscopic marine life and sometimes jellyfish cling to the rope. A pair of gloves will come in handy on such occasions but remember to take them off during the dive, keeping with the notion: Look, but don't touch. The dive boat will remain stationary at the dive site while divers are in the water but a safety sausage should be part of every diver's gear in case you are a little too adventurous and leave your group behind, something that should not happen.

Given the remoteness of many dive sites and consequential distance to hyperbaric chambers and medical facilities, as well as the high number of dives that may be done during the day, depth limits and dive times (NDL) must be respected and complied with. The use of dive computers or dive tables is advised. In addition, experience and common sense are required in order for you to enjoy exploring the wonders of Malaysia's underwater world.

WEATHER

Malaysia is a tropical country with a warm and humid climate all year round. Temperatures tend to range from 28° to 34° Centigrade during the day and 18° to 20° Centigrade at night. Malaysia does not experience severe storms that last for days or typhoons.

The country does, however, experience monsoon seasons. The northeast monsoon is characterised by steady northeast winds that blow from mid-November until early March. During this period, widespread heavy rain lasting 2 to 3 days falls over the east coast states of Peninsular Malaysia and the coastal areas of Sarawak and the east coast of Sabah. About three to four such spells usually occur throughout the monsoon season. In between these heavy rain spells, the weather is relatively fair. In November and early December, the west coast of Peninsular Malaysia frequently experiences thunderstorms in the afternoon.

The monsoon rains usually begin after the first week of November over the states of Kelantan and Terengganu while the state of Pahang and east Johor usually receive heavy rainfall in December and early January. From mid-January, the weather becomes drier over Peninsular Malaysia. On occasion, during the months of November and December, strong northeast winds can cause a spillover of rain across the west coast where widespread rain can last for a few hours.

In both Sarawak and Sabah, heavy rain spells usually occur between late December and early February.

The inter-monsoon season on the west coast of the peninsula lasts from April to May. It is punctuated by occasional storms and heavy rainfall in the late afternoon. During the same period, Sarawak and Sabah typically enjoy very dry and hot weather. On occasion, this weather causes a haze to form over inland areas.

The southwest monsoon, lasting from July to September, brings windy conditions to the west coast of the peninsula with frequent rainfall in the late afternoon.

To get current information about Malaysia's weather and marine conditions, go to: www.kjc.gov.my/english/weather/forecast/ship.html

ECO-FRIENDLY SCUBA DIVING

Diving in Malaysia

- Every diver should practise low impact diving techniques, or as the saying goes: Take only pictures, leave only bubbles.

- Securely fasten equipment such as gauges, octopus (spare regulator), cameras, etc.

- Check for correct buoyancy and make adjustments during your descent and not when you have already hit corals.

- Move slowly and carefully. Know where you are in relation to your surroundings.

- Do not touch any corals with your fins or stir up sediment.

- Do not hold onto corals. If it really is necessary for you to do so, hold onto dead coral.

- Do not touch underwater plants or animals, including corals.

- Do not chase, ride or block the path of animals such as turtles, dolphins or whales.

Do not collect any souvenirs, living or dead.

 Do not feed any marine animals.

 During night dives and while taking photographs, take care of your buoyancy.

Key to Dive Sites
Dive Rating
Rationale for rating: Visibility and water colour, pollution (e.g. suspended solids), consistency of biodiversity and density, topography (walls, boulders, dive-thrus, currents, entry and exit) and damage to the reef.

Symbol	Rating
⌐	poor, don't waste your air
⌐ ⌐	fair
⌐ ⌐ ⌐	good
⌐ ⌐ ⌐ ⌐	very good
⌐ ⌐ ⌐ ⌐ ⌐	excellent; addictive; go back for more

Photo Rating
Rationale for rating: Diversity and density of marine life and corresponding photo opportunities, unique encounters, visibility, water quality and currents.

Symbol	Rating
1	poor; don't waste your film or battery
2	fair
3	good
4	very good
5	excellent; bring lots of film and memory cards

PENINSULAR MALAYSIA, SABAH AND SARAWAK

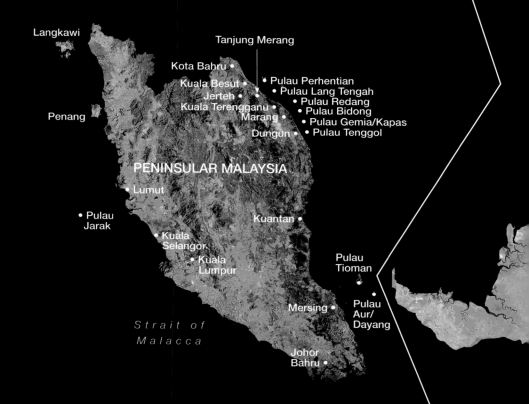

Langkawi

Tanjung Merang

Kota Bahru •

Kuala Besut •
Jerteh •
Kuala Terengganu •
Marang •
Dungun •

• Pulau Perhentian
• Pulau Lang Tengah
• Pulau Redang
• Pulau Bidong
• Pulau Gemia/Kapas
• Pulau Tenggol

Penang

PENINSULAR MALAYSIA

• Lumut

• Pulau
Jarak

Kuantan •

• Kuala
Selangor

• Kuala
Lumpur

Pulau
Tioman

Mersing •

Pulau
Aur/
Dayang

*Strait of
Malacca*

Johor
Bahru •

SOUTH CHINA
SEA

Layang-Layang

SULU SEA

Tunku
Abdul Rahman
Marine Park

Pulau
Lankayan

Kota
Kinabalu

Sandakan

Pulau
Labuan

SABAH

Pulau
Mataking

Miri

Tawau

Semporna

Pulau
Mabul

Pulau
Kapalai

SARAWAK

Pulau
Sipadan

CELEBES SEA

N

PULAU REDANG

Coordinates: 05.46.1N, 103.01.5E

Left: Lush and brightly coloured soft corals (*Dendronephthya* and *Siphonogorgia*) feeding in the nutrient-rich currents of the Redang archipelago

Inset: A school of yellow-band fusiliers (*Pterocaesio chrysozona*)

Pulau Redang is located 22 kilometres east of the coastal village of Tanjung Merang, 26 kilometres east-southeast of Pulau Perhentian and 45 kilometres north-northeast of Kuala Terengganu, the state capital of Terengganu. It is the main island in the small archipelago known as Redang. The archipelago also includes Pulau Pinang and the islets of Pulau Kerengga Besar, Pulau Kerengga Kecil, Pulau Paku Besar, Pulau Paku Kecil, Pulau Ekor Tebu, Pulau Ling and Pulau Lima.

The Redang archipelago makes up the Pulau Redang Marine Park. The park was gazetted in 1994 and is a protected zone with reefs that have one of the best coral and marine ecosystems in Peninsular Malaysia. The boundary of Pulau Redang Marine Park is established by a line linking all points 2 nautical miles from the shores of Pulau Redang, Pulau Lima, Pulau Ekor Tebu and Pulau Pinang. Measuring approximately 7 kilometres by 6 kilometres, Pulau Redang is the largest island in the marine park.

Historically, the first settlers of Pulau Redang are believed to have been the Bugis, seafaring gypsies from the Celebes Sea, who established their first village at Telok Kalong but later moved to Pulau Pinang (now the location of Pulau Redang Marine Park Centre). Kampung Air (Water Village) on Pulau Redang was home to about 300 families thought to be descended from the original Bugis settlers. When the original village was torn down in 2001, some families moved to the mainland while others chose to relocate to a new village inland and either continued with their traditional fishing-related lifestyle or looked for work at the resorts.

Geologically, Pulau Redang is made up primarily of granite and sedimentary rocks. Soil cover is generally thin and unsuitable for agriculture, except around the Sungei Redang basin and the summit of Bukit Besar, the island's highest peak at 359 metres.

Sungei Redang, the main river, divides the island. It flows north to south and enters the sea opposite Pulau Redang Marine Park Centre. The river is flanked by two ridges and mangroves are present along the tidal zone of its estuary.

The island's interior is covered with thick vegetation comprising mainly *shorea* forests in the west and *dipterocarp* forests in the east. Coconut trees line the sandy shores. Pristine sandy beaches can be found along Teluk Kalong and Pasir Panjang (Long Beach) in the east, Chagar Hutang and Teluk Dalam in the north and Mak Kepit and Mak Simpan in the west. Rocky outcrops, steep walls, cliffs, caves and grottos dominate the remainder of the coastline. Small reptiles and amphibians such as snakes, monitor lizards and frogs; small mammals such as macaque monkeys, bats and mouse deer; and more than 50 species of bird make up the fauna of the island.

100 species of reef and pelagic fish as well as green turtles and hawksbill turtles.

The waters exhibit wide and diverse types of dive sites. Underwater visibility is generally good, ranging from 10 to 20 metres, and water temperatures are between 27° and 29° Centigrade.

The park's abundance of well-scouted dive sites offers divers the opportunity to choose what to explore, be it the abundant coral reefs, pelagic species or macro life forms.

Left: A lush gorgonian sea fan (*Subergorgia*) perched on a rocky reef outcrop

Redang has experienced rapid development over the past decade and was made intensely popular by the 2000 Hong Kong motion picture *Summer Holiday,* or *Mo Mo Cha*. Resorts covering the entire spectrum from luxurious to basic now occupy most of Pasir Panjang and Teluk Kalong beaches on the eastern coastline. At weekends and on public holidays, the island experiences a large influx of visitors so it is advisable to make reservations in advance.

Diving Pulau Redang

The reefs of the Redang archipelago are part of the Indo-West Pacific region, an area in which faunal diversity exceeds that of other tropical regions. The reef-building coral species number more than 500 and many faunal families, such as the beautiful giant clam, are not found elsewhere. The marine ecosystem is also home to over

Pulau Redang Endangered?

In recent years, the media has repeatedly reported that Pulau Redang and its ecosystem is experiencing widespread destruction and excessive development. This, however, does not necessarily reflect a balanced view. Although some developments, climatic phenomena like *El Niño* and the infestation of predators such as crown-of-thorns starfish have stressed and continue to stress the healthy balance of the ecosystem, concerted efforts and plans by the public and private sectors, especially among the local resort and dive operators, are being formulated and implemented to preserve one of Malaysia's best marine environments. Some of these initiatives include zoning dive and snorkel sites, responsible waste disposal, restricting the construction of jetties and resorts, education and public awareness campaigns, frequent clean-ups and replanting corals.

Getting There

The gateway to Pulau Redang is Kuala Terengganu and both Malaysia Airlines (www.malaysiaairlines.com) and AirAsia (www.airasia.com) operate daily flights there. The transfer from Sultan Mahmud Airport to the coastal village of Tanjung Merang takes about 30 minutes.

If you are driving, make your way to Kuala Terengganu via the east coast highway and then proceed to Tanjung Merang. Ample secure parking is available at the ferry terminal at a reasonable rate. Alternatively, Transnasional operates two daily air-conditioned coach services. The transfer to Tanjung Merang takes about 30 minutes.

The boat/ferry services to Pulau Redang run from Tanjung Merang Jetty and take about 45 minutes. Normally the boats depart for Pulau Redang and return before noon. However, each resort has its own boat transfer schedule depending on sea and weather conditions.

Accommodation

Berjaya Redang Beach Resort
Pulau Redang, PO Box 126, Main Post Office
20928 Kuala Terengganu, Terengganu
Tel: (60) 9 697 3988
Fax: (60) 9 697 3899
Email: reserdept@b-redang.com.my
Website: www.berjayaresorts.com.my/redang-beach/info.html

Coral Redang Island Resort
Kuala Terengganu Office: 9 Jalan Kampong Dalam
20100 Kuala Terengganu, Terengganu
Tel: (60) 9 692 0110 / (60) 9 690 2111
Fax: (60) 9 690 2112
Email: crir@tm.net.my
Website: www.coralredang.com.my

Redang Pelangi Resort
Kuala Terengganu Office: 2A Jalan Syed Hussin
20100 Kuala Terengganu, Terengganu
Tel: (60) 9 624 2158
Fax: (60) 9 623 5202
Email: reservation@redangpelangi.com
Website: www.redangpelangi.com

Laguna Redang Island Resort
Pasir Panjang, Pulau Redang
Tel: (60) 9 697 7888
Fax: (60) 9 697 8999
Email: enquiry@lagunaredang.com.my
Website: www.lagunaredang.com.my

Redang Camping Adventure
Available at Teluk Kalong and Pasir Panjang beaches

Redang Bay Resort
Kuala Terengganu Office: 139 Jalan Bandar
20100 Kuala Terengganu, Terengganu
Tel: (60) 9 620 3200
Fax: (60) 9 624 2048
Email: reservation@redangbay.com.my
Website: www.redangbay.com.my

Redang Lagoon Chalet
Kuala Terengganu Office: 326 Taman Sri Jaya
21300 Kuala Terengganu, Terengganu
Tel: (60) 9 666 5020
Fax: (60) 9 666 5018
Email: admin@redanglagoon.com
Website: www.redanglagoon.com

Redang Beach Resort
Kuala Terengganu Office: 77B Jalan Sultan Sulaiman
20100 Kuala Terengganu, Terengganu
Tel: (60) 9 623 8188
Fax: (60) 9 623 0225
Email: thw@tm.net.my
Website: www.redang.com.my

Redang Kalong Resort
Kuala Terengganu Office: 57 Jalan Sultan Zainal Abidin
20000 Kuala Terengganu, Terengganu
Tel: (60) 9 622 1691 / (60) 9 622 8186
Fax: (60) 9 622 8186
Email: enquiry@redangkalong.com
Website: www.redangkalong.com

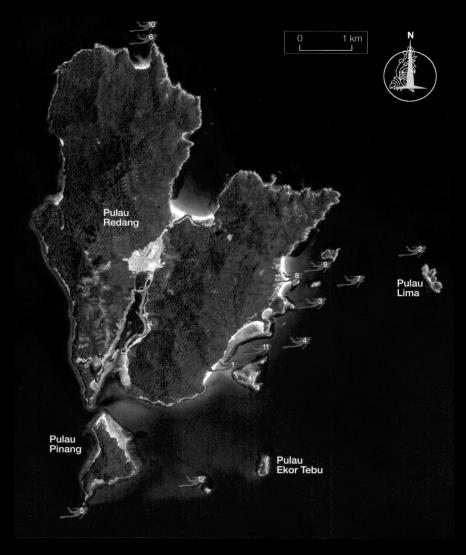

0   1 km

N

Pulau
Redang

Pulau
Lima

Pulau
Pinang

Pulau
Ekor Tebu

Key for Dive Sites

1: Steven Stone	5: Terumbu Kili	9: Pulau Paku
2: Big Mount	6: Tanjong Tokong	10: Whale Mount
3: Mak Cantik	7: Cow Reef	11: Pulau Kerengga
4: Mini Mount	8: Tanjung Tengah (House Reef)	12: Pulau Ling

Steven Stone

Location: 05.44.52N, 103.01.05E

Average depth: 15 m

Maximum depth: 17 m

Dive rating: 🐋 🐋 🐋 🐋

Photo rating: 4, Macro

Unique features: Lionfish, moray eels, stonefish, a host of macro life

Take note: Usually not enough film

Hazards: None

A 10-minute boat ride from Redang Bay Resort on Pasir Panjang Beach, Steven Stone is an innocent-looking site located between Pulau Redang and Pulau Kerengga Besar. However, 17 metres below the surface is a site home to a surprising variety of species. It is considered by many to be one of the best dives for those with patience and an eye for detail.

The site is essentially a patch reef structure surrounded by four smaller mounds that feature hard and encrusting corals, whip corals and boulders. The many crevices and gaps within the boulders are home to moray, honeycomb and yellow eels while stonefish, scorpionfish, crocodile fish and blue-spotted rays camouflage themselves on the sandy seabed, waiting for unsuspecting prey. Numerous nudibranchs, the very shy yellow boxfish, juvenile porcupinefish, pufferfish and juvenile white-tip and nurse sharks can also be found. Cleaner shrimps offer their services to the multitude of inhabitants and, with a little bit of patience, you may get a good manicure yourself.

Leaving the main reef, make your way across the sandy seafloor for about 20 metres (keep a lookout for well-camouflaged blue-spotted rays and stingrays along the way) until you reach a group of boulders colonised by whip corals. Although schools of yellow snappers are common, the numerous motionless zebra lionfish which seem to be resident here are the main attraction. Careful buoyancy control is prudent as it is very easy to get too close and into harm's way.

Steven Stone is definitely a site that should be dived more than once as one dive alone does not allow you to explore the multitude of marine life gathered here.

1: A yellow-margined moray eel (*Gymnothorax flavimarginatus*)

2: The common lionfish (*Pterois volitans*)–beware the beauty so fraught with danger

3: A small scorpionfish (*Scorpaenopsis oxycephalus*) patiently lying in wait for prey

4: A cleaner shrimp (*Urocardidella antonbruunii*) 'on station' waiting for patrons

1

2

3

4

Big Mount

Location: 05.46.36N, 103.03.30E

Average depth: 20 m

Maximum depth: 38 m

Dive rating: 🐊 🐊 🐊

Photo rating: 3, Wide angle

Unique features: Large black coral, soft coral, jacks, barracudas

Hazards: Strong current can challenge the less experienced diver

Off the northern tip of Pulau Lima and marked by a dive site marker buoy, the sea mount's huge boulders and pinnacle reach 10 metres below the surface on the landward side and have a bottom depth in excess of 40 metres. The orientation of the boulders is roughly in an east-west direction. Tidal movements can cause strong currents at this site and novice divers may be challenged.

The lower regions and sandy bottom feature large black coral swaying majestically in the current. A large variety of soft corals encrust the large boulders at progressively shallower depths in addition to whip corals, sea fans, gorgonians, nudibranchs, symbiotic anemone clownfish, damselfish, moray eels, schools of yellow-tail snappers and a host of other macro life. Due to the prevailing stronger current,

schools of big-eyed jacks, barracudas and inquisitive batfish are the norm as are occasional eagle rays, rock groupers, wrasses and black-tip sharks. This is a much sought-after site with frequent sightings of whale sharks passing through this nutrient-rich area during the months of June and July.

1: Soft coral (*Dendronephthya*) colourfully decorating a rocky outcrop

2: Barrel sponge (*Haplosclerida*) covered with sea cucumbers (*Opheodesoma*), its source of nutrition

3: A colourful nudibranch (*Flabellina rubrolineata*), a much sought-after photographic subject

4: Soft coral (*Siphonogorgia*) perched on the fringing reef

5: A school of cardinalfish (*Apogonidae*)

6: Majestic and gravity-defying table coral (*Acropora latistella*)

Mak Cantik

Location: 05.45.57N, 103.02.18E

Average depth: 15 m

Maximum depth: 19 m

Dive rating: 🦈🦈🦈🦈

Photo rating: 4, Wide angle; 4, Macro for night dives

Unique features: Stingrays, sharks, acroporus, excellent night dives

Take note: Addictive—you will come back for more!

Hazards: None

1

A 10-minute boat ride from Redang Bay Resort on Pasir Panjang Beach, Mak Cantik is a richly populated and beautiful submerged reef. The dive starts by descending along the marker buoy line to around 19 metres where you will reach the sandy bottom that surrounds the reef. The boulders and hard corals demarcating the reef are home to boxfish, pufferfish, flat heads, moray eels, lionfish and a variety of nudibranchs. Grey stingrays, blue-spotted rays and white-tip reef sharks patrol the reef fringes.

A generally dense growth of acroporus, hard and soft corals, sponges and sea fans is interrupted by some leftover bald patches as a result of coral bleaching. Yellow snappers, schools of yellowtail barracudas,

Once you have circumvented the reef, which should take about 25 minutes, ascend to the upper portion of the reef.

2

1: A star puffer (*Arothron stellatus*) and a blue-ringed angelfish (*Pomacanthus annularis*) living in peaceful coexistence

2: A green turtle (*Chelonia mydas*) that bears the marks of a close encounter with a motor boat

3: A colourful nudibranch (*Chromodorididae ooi*)

jacks, the occasional green turtle, devil fish, a lone great barracuda, schools of parrotfish and resident black-tip and white-tip reef sharks are common sights.

Not to be missed is a night dive at Mak Cantik, a highlight and must of any visit to Pulau Redang. If a dive during the day is already a rewarding experience, the reef's nocturnal residents and predators are truly spectacular to observe. The dive light will reveal an incessant variety of species and activities from hunting white-tip reef sharks,

crustaceans trying to escape becoming the next meal for the numerous blue-spotted rays and stingrays and sleeping parrotfish, stonefish and crocodile fish to hermit and decorator crabs blending into the surrounding corals. Don't forget to peek into the caves for a pleasant surprise— your light may catch the tail of a magnificent turquoise bumphead. If you switch off your light during the safety stop and wave your hands, the darkness will come alive with countless silvery plankton particles.

Mini Mount

Location: 05.45.29N, 103.02.06E

Average depth: 15 m

Maximum depth: 19 m

Dive rating: 🤿 🤿 🤿

Photo rating: 4, Wide angle during the day; 4, Macro for night dives

Unique features: Featherstars, soft corals, nurse sharks, white-tip sharks, night dive

Hazards: None

Located southwest of Pulau Lima, this site is a smaller version of Big Mount. The boulders go down to a maximum depth of 20 metres. Submerged rocks and boulders are topped with prolific featherstars and soft corals. Occasional gorgonian fans and large sea fans cling to the granite faces. The sandy bottom is populated by blue-spotted stingrays and star puffers, yellowtail barracudas and resting nurse and white-tip sharks.

Night dives are an experience not to be missed. Hermit and decorator crabs, schools of bumphead parrotfish frolicking among the corals, cleaner shrimps, lionfish, devil fish, flatheads and delightfully colourful nudibranchs are present in significant numbers.

You should exercise good buoyancy control to stay clear of the fire corals and hydroids.

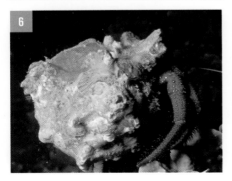

1: A decorator crab (*Camposcia retusa*), one of many nocturnally active crustaceans

2: A tiger cowry (*Cypraea tigris*), a member of the gastropod species

3: Graceful tube anemone feeding in the current

4: A juvenile common lionfish (*Pterois volitans*) waiting for unsuspecting prey

5: Cleaner shrimp (*Stenopus hispidus*) 'on station'

6: A hermit crab (*Dardanus megistus*) on its nightly foray into the reef

Terumbu Kili

Location: 05.43.46N, 102.59.46E

Average depth: 15 m

Maximum depth: 22 m

Dive rating: ✈ ✈ ✈

Photo rating: 3, Wide angle

Unique features: Shoals of diverse reef fish, gorgonians, sea fans

Hazards: None

This reef is in the channel between Pulau Pinang and a surface-breaking rock at the southernmost tip of Pulau Redang. It is accessible from Redang Bay Resort in 15 minutes. Descending to the sandy bottom at a depth of 22 metres, the assembly of large rocks and boulders is covered by vividly coloured soft and encrusting corals, gorgonian sea fans and featherstars while patches of sea anemones, reminiscent of flowerpots, are common on the sandy expanse.

Crossing the channel (a good swim against the current) will bring you to the reef slope of Pulau Pinang. This hosts a population of diverse reef life such as snappers, lionfish, diamond fish, hawksbill turtles, moray eels, groupers, barracudas, barramundi cod, black-tip reef sharks, bumphead parrotfish, scorpionfish and giant clams.

1: Intricately designed coral (*Tubastrea micrantha*)

2: The nutrient-rich waters of the channel account for the rich growth of soft corals (*Siphonogorgia* sp.).

3: Split-banded cardinalfish (*Apogon compressus*) among an assortment of soft and whip corals

4: A variety of encrusting and soft corals

Tanjong Tokong

Location: 05.49.30N, 103.00.45E

Average depth: 15 m

Maximum depth: 28 m

Dive rating:

Photo rating: 3, Wide angle

Unique features: Gorgonians, sea fans, napoleon wrasse, sharks, turtles

Hazards: The occasional thermocline makes for a 'refreshing' dive

The boat ride to Tanjong Tokong passes a coastline dominated by rocky outcrops, steep walls, cliffs, caves and grottos. Located at the northernmost tip of Pulau Redang and adjacent to Turtle Bay, this site is characterised by a jumble of large boulders covered in large gorgonians and sea fans. Green turtles, trevallies, tuna, a lone napoleon wrasse, barramundi cod, titan triggerfish, emperorfish and unicorn fish are often sighted. At the lower region of around 25 to 30 metres, marble rays and white-tip reef sharks patrol the edge of the reef. During a thermocline, snappers and jacks use the difference in water temperature to shoot up from the lower region, making for a spectacular display.

1: A delicate sea whip (*Junceella fragilis*) surrounded by a cloud of nose-spot cardinalfish (*Rhabdamia cypselura*)

2: An assembly of soft corals (*Dendronephthya*)–a garden in perfect harmony

Facing page: This luxuriant growth of soft coral (*Siphonogorgia*) provides a habitat for a school of golden sweepers (*Parapriacanthus ransonneti*).

Cow Reef

Location: 05.45.30N, 103.01.56E

Average depth: 18 m

Maximum depth: 20 m

Dive rating: 🤿 🤿 🤿

Photo rating: 3, Macro

Unique features: Panda clownfish, pavo razorfish, sand divers

Hazards: None

Located halfway between Pulau Redang and Pulau Lima, the featureless flat sandy bottom at 16 to 18 metres does not appear to be a worthwhile dive destination. However, upon closer inspection, a variety of marine creatures such as gobies, emperor shrimps, the rare pavo razorfish, the

juvenile cuttlefish, sand divers and seapens make the seabed come alive. The highlight of this site is a family of rare and very shy panda clownfish living among anemones and anemone shrimps. You will have to be patient and approach the clownfish slowly as they disappear into the depth of an anemone at the slightest disturbance and the wait for their reappearance can be rather lengthy. Other species you will encounter are lionfish, sea cucumbers and the occasional lone barracuda.

4

1: A solitary seapen (*Pteroeides*)

2: A starfish shrimp (*Periclimenes soror*), which usually forms a symbiotic relationship with its host species

3: A polyclad flatworm (*Thysanozoon* sp.) sliding across a self-secreted mat of mucus

4: Panda clownfish (*Amphiprion polymnus*) found on the sandy channels between reefs

Tanjung Tengah
(House Reef)

Location: 05.46.18N, 103.01.57E

Average depth: 15 m

Maximum depth: 17 m

Dive rating:

Photo rating: 3, Wide angle

Unique features: Juvenile reef fish, sharks, stingrays

Hazards: None

Tanjung Tengah is the house reef and training site of Redang Bay Resort. It offers easy dives in clear waters as well as opportunities for snorkelling. During low tide, a sandbank connects the island to Pulau Redang and it is a favourite spot to watch the sunset.

Entry to the reef is from the beach. Depending on the prevailing current, you will start the dive either in front of Redang Laguna Resort or on the doorstep of the Redang Bay dive centre. This fringing reef can be circumvented in about 45 minutes at a maximum depth of about 12 metres. Acroporus corals predominate the shallower part of the reef while boulders

and rocks with soft corals and vividly coloured featherstars cover the deeper end. Schools of rabbitfish, diamond fish and yellowtail snappers flit from boulder to boulder. Stingrays and blue-spotted ribbontail rays getting a good clean from the ever compliant cleaner wrasses as well as moray eels, bumphead parrotfish and groupers add to the diversity and colour of this site. It is also a nursery for reef fish and juvenile nurse sharks.

Although the construction of the jetty and constant snorkelling activities have caused the reef to deteriorate somewhat, it is still a worthwhile and easy dive.

1: Schooling wideband fusiliers (*Pterocaesio lativitata*) among encrusting corals and featherstars

2: A coral arrangement (*Pachyseris foliosa*)

Other notable dive sites

Pulau Paku is a small, wooded island northeast of Redang Bay. It is surrounded by a shallow (8- to 12-metre) fringing reef that features a nice seascape and reef fish.

Whale Mount offers a deeper dive (15–35 metres) and is situated north of Tanjung Tokong. It features large gorgonians and sea fans. Whale sharks may also be seen. This site is seasonally dependent.

Pulau Kerengga, a shallow reef (10–14 metres), encircles a rocky outcrop where you might encounter humphead parrotfish, schools of yellowtail snappers, golden trevallies and barracudas while a shovelnose shark might mingle occasionally with stingrays at the sandy bottom.

Pulau Ling is famed for two massive, mushroom-shaped coral heads believed to be the largest coral structures on the east coast of Peninsular Malaysia. The larger of the two has a circumference of about 25 metres and a height of 12 metres while the smaller one is 24 metres and 10 metres, respectively. The deep overhangs at the bases of this porite support the luxuriant growth of brilliantly coloured daisy coral and is home to a variety of fish. The dive is 10 to 18 metres.

1: Colourful soft coral (*Echinigorgia*) perched on a rocky outcrop

2: A gorgonian fan (*Subergorgia mollis*) projecting all its splendour from the reef's surface

Facing page: Lush soft coral (*Siphonogorgia* sp.)

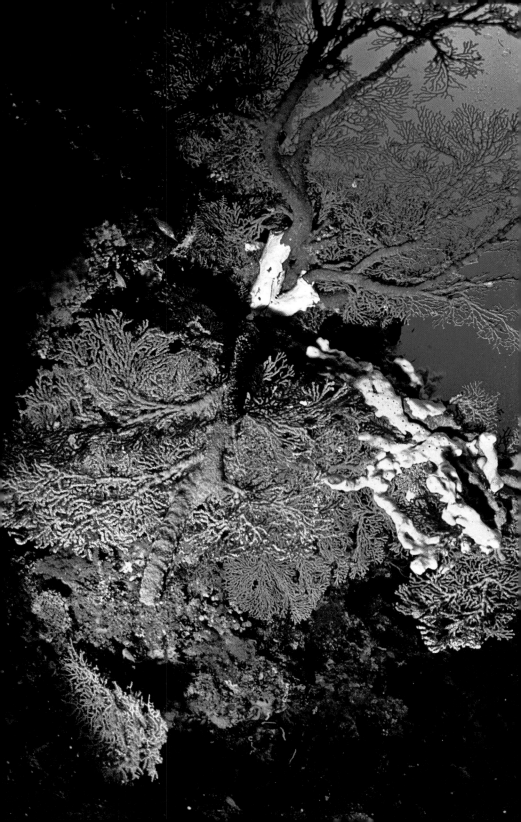

PULAU PERHENTIAN

Coordinates: 05.48.40N, 103.00.0E

Left: Magnificent soft corals (*Siphonogorgia* sp.) adjoining the reef slopes of Pulau Perhentian

Inset: The very ornate Christmas tree worm (*Spirobranchus giganteus*) is a common sight on most reefs.

Located 25 kilometres off the coast of Kelantan, Pulau Perhentian is the northernmost island group off the east coast of Peninsular Malaysia. It also forms part of Terengganu Marine Park. There are nine islands in the small archipelago: two inhabited islands called Pulau Perhentian Besar (Big Stopover Island) and Pulau Perhentian Kecil (Small Stopover Island) and seven islets.

Geologically, the islands feature granite and sedimentary rock with a dense coverage of forest that gives way to palm tree fringed sandy beaches and bays which break the monotony of the rocky coastlines. Reptiles and amphibians including snakes, monitor lizards and frogs; small mammals such as macaque monkeys, bats and mouse deer; and a variety of species of bird make up the fauna of the islands.

The waters surrounding the islands once teemed with a rich variety of marine life but these waters have degraded and become polluted in recent years. Still, divers continue to visit the archipelago to dive the boulder-strewn seabeds and see large soft corals, schools of pelagic species and nocturnal seashells that are sometimes spotted in the channel between the two main islands.

Although both islands lack comprehensive infrastructure, they have become much sought-after destinations for tourists, foreign and local alike. Virtually overnight, A-huts, chalets and beach cafés, many of which have been built in a haphazard manner, have appeared over the past few years to meet the growing demand. Although the capacity of rooms has increased manifold, advance booking is recommended during the holiday season (July/August) and around public holidays.

Resorts on Pulau Perhentian Besar are clustered around Teluk Pauh and Teluk Dalam. Teluk Pauh is located on the west coast and is a half-moon shaped bay with a sandy beach, clear waters and good coral coverage along the reef fringes. Teluk Dalam in the southeastern corner of

the island is a sheltered bay with a nice sandy beach and shallow waters although the corals here have experienced widespread destruction.

With its white sandy beach and clear shallow waters, Pasir Panjang (Long Beach) is the most popular beach on Pulau Perhentian Kecil. Visitors who have been here in the past, however, should no longer expect a peaceful, deserted beach and may be disappointed with the haphazard way in which Long Beach has been developed. It is almost completely covered with chalets, huts, restaurants and cafés, although it still retains some of its rustic beauty. The atmosphere is very much determined by the

1: A nudibranch (*Phyllidia varicosa*), a much sought-after and an always willing photographic subject

2: A colony of magnificent sea anemones (*Heteractis magifica*) feeding on planktonic plants

3 & 4: Ascidians (*Didemnum molle* and *Rhopalaea crassa*), efficient filter feeders in reefs and common in all marine habitats

clientele (laid-back, twenty-something backpackers). During spring tides, the waves at Long Beach can be quite high. As it does not have a jetty, boats may not be able to land so you may have to walk 15 minutes from Teluk Aur on the opposite side of the island to get there. Kampung Pasir Hantu in the southeast is the only village on the island and comprises a cluster of wooden houses, a police station, a school, a clinic and a mosque.

Diving Pulau Perhentian

The fringing reefs of the Perhentian islands are a blend of hard coral species with patches of *Dendronephthya* soft corals, whip corals and sponges growing on boulders. The seascape terrain is either gentle slopes or plunging granite boulders, with most dive sites accessible by boat. Currents around the reefs are usually manageable, with the submerged reefs washed by slightly stronger currents.

Visibility underwater is generally good, from 10 to 20 metres, but can get a little poor mid season. The water temperature is between 27° and 29° Centigrade.

The waters exhibit wide and diverse types of dive sites. Mooring buoys mark the most popular dive sites within the marine park zone. There are also a number of snorkelling sites. However, the stress from too many snorkellers and the rampant development of resorts and corresponding pollution on land and in the sea are having a marked effect on the health of the reef. A similar effect can be observed at the dive sites close to the shore and even at some of the more distant locations. Poor water quality has led to an infestation of reef predatory species such as sea urchins and crown-of-thorns starfish.

Besides the numerous independent operators that have set up shop on the islands, almost every resort has a dive centre. It is essential that you check that the operator complies with standard safety regulations and has well-maintained equipment, including the dive boat.

Getting There

To get to Pulau Perhentian, you need to make your way to the fishing village of Kuala Besut. Malaysia Airlines (www.malaysiaairlines.com) and AirAsia (www.airasia.com) operate daily flights from Kuala Lumpur International Airport (KLIA) to Sultan Mahmud Airport in Kuala Terengganu and Kota Bahru Airport. It should be noted that Kota Bahru Airport is nearer to Kuala Besut. Taxis for the onward journey to Kuala Besut are available from both airports, taking about 70 minutes from Sultan Mahmud Airport and 50 minutes from Kota Bahru Airport.

If you take the express bus, stop at the small town of Jerteh and take an onward bus or taxi to Kuala Besut. Boats to Pulau Perhentian leave from Kuala Besut Jetty. The slow boat takes about 90 minutes while speedboat takes about 30 minutes.

Accommodation

ON PULAU PERHENTIAN BESAR

Flora Bay Resort
Pantai Teluk Dalam
Pulau Perhentian Besar
22300 Besut, Terengganu
Tel: (60) 9 697 7266 / (6) 013 943 6031
Email: florabay@tm.net.my
Website: www.florabayresort.com

Perhentian Island Resort
Daerah Besut
Pulau Perhentian Besar
22200 Besut, Terengganu
Tel: (60) 10 903 0100
Fax: (60) 10 903 0106
Website: www.jaring.my/perhentian

Tuna Bay Island Resort
Management Office: 120 Jalan Bewar
22300 Besut, Terengganu
Tel: (60) 9 697 9779 / (60) 9 699 1779
Fax: (60) 9 690 4863
Email: survivor@tunabay.com.my
Website: tunabay.com.my

ON PULAU PERHENTIAN KECIL
Bubu Long Beach Resort
Kuala Besut Sales Office: BUBU Inn
Jalan Pantai, Kuala Besut
22300 Besut, Terengganu
Tel: (60) 3 2078 0080 / (60) 9 697 8888
Fax: (60) 3 2072 0080 / (60) 9 697 5080
Email: info@buburesort.com.my
Website: www.buburesort.com.my

Maya Beach Resort
Coral Bay (Teluk Aur)
Pulau Perhentian Kecil
Terengganu
Tel: (6) 019 964 3311
Tel (reservations): (6) 019 937 9136
Email: mayabeachresort@yahoo.com
Website: www.mayaresort.now.nu/

Suria Perhentian Dive Resort
Coral Bay (Teluk Aur)
Pulau Perhentian Kecil
Terengganu
Tel: (60) 9 697 7960
Fax: (60) 11 970 712
Email: maxcarry@tm.net.my
Website: www.suriaperhentian.com

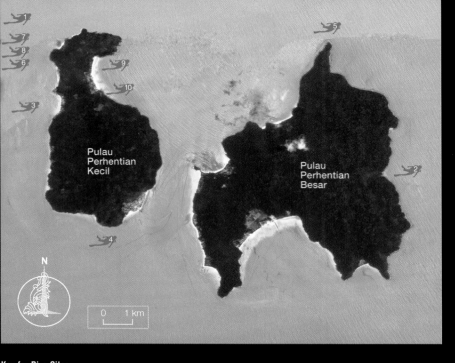

Key for Dive Sites

1: Tokong Laut	5: Tanjung Besi	9: Teluk Kerma
2: Terumbu Tiga	6: Pulau Serenggeh	10: Batu Nisan
3: Pasir Kerangi	7: Pulau Susu Dara Besar	
4: Pasir Tani	8: Pulau Susu Dara Kecil	

Tokong Laut

Location: 05.48.59N, 103.00.33E

Average depth: 15 m

Maximum depth: 30 m

Dive rating: 🤿 🤿 🤿

Photo rating: 3, Wide angle

Unique features: Soft corals, trevallies, jacks, barracudas, green turtles

Hazards: Mild to strong currents with waves on the north-facing side

Part of the group of rocky islets and outcrops northwest of Pulau Perhentian Kecil, Tokong Laut is characterised by a boulder terrain that descends to a depth of about 30 metres. Spectacular colourful soft corals in the upper region and a healthy growth of black coral, large gorgonians and sea fans sprout in the deeper region of the site among the valley-like gaps between the rocks. Green turtles, trevallies, tuna, a lone napoleon wrasse, barramundi cod, emperor and titan triggerfish, emperorfish, unicorn fish, jacks, barracudas, kingfish, black-tip sharks, nurse sharks and, depending on the season, whale sharks can be sighted. At

the lower region of around 25 to 30 metres, marble rays and white-tip reef sharks patrol the edge of the reef. If you venture to the sandy bottom, occasional tube sponges, sea whips, sea cucumbers, sea stars and clusters of sea urchins round up the picture of this diverse site.

As the north-facing side of the islet is exposed to the open sea and occasional larger waves, entry and exit at the calmer southern side is advisable.

Facing page: A breathtaking reef densely populated with a variety of soft corals

Left: Lush, gravity-defying soft coral (*Tubastrea micrantha*) feeding in the current

Terumbu Tiga

Location: 05.53.54N, 102.46.22E

Average depth: 15 m

Maximum depth: 22 m

Dive rating: 🐟 🐟 🐟 🐟

Photo rating: 4, Wide angle

Unique features: Shoals of trevallies, snappers, good soft coral cover

Hazards: Can experience strong currents and swell

Terumbu Tiga is a dive site that should not be missed while diving the Perhentian islands. Located at the centre of the eastern side of Pulau Perhentian Besar, three large boulders jutting out of the sea mark the entry point to the site. The jumble of large boulders covered with hard and soft corals including soft tree corals, *Acropora*, cup corals and sponges tapers off to a sandy bottom at about 22 metres. Careful observation will reveal a diverse range of macro life forms such as molluscs, shrimps and nudibranchs. Shoals of trevallies, snappers and parrotfish are ever present as are sea anemones and clownfish, large groupers, spotted rays, different types of angelfish, butterflyfish, wrasses and spotted sweetlips. A prominent feature are the numerous and colourful *Dendronephthya* soft corals, large white gorgonian sea fans, sea whips and black corals. The small boulders and rocks on the sandy patches are home to colourful Christmas tree worms, sea stars, lizardfish, pufferfish, scorpionfish, gobies and sea cucumbers. Due to the strong nutrient-rich current, it is not uncommon to spot white-tip reef sharks and the occasional turtle.

Above: Chevron barracudas (*Sphyraena genie*) drifting in the current

Pasir Kerangi

Location: Southwestern edge of Pulau Perhentian Kecil

Average depth: 18 m

Maximum depth: 18 m

Dive rating: 🐟 🐟

Photo rating: 3, Macro

Unique features: PVC pipe reef, growth of corals and sponges, diverse range of reef fish

Hazards: Visibility can be marginal

In an effort to stimulate reef formation on the western fringes of Pulau Perhentian Kecil, the Fisheries Department constructed an artificial reef made out of PVC pipes in 1991. With constant currents bringing in nutrients, this artificial reef has become a rich habitat for large colourful soft corals and sponges. Schools of fusiliers, yellowtail snappers, damselfish, groupers and butterflyfish have also made this reef their home. Porcupinefish and black-spotted pufferfish dart in and out of the structures while flatworms, nudibranchs, lionfish and moray eels play hide and seek. Visibility can, at times, be a meagre 5 to 7 metres.

Tanjung Besi

Location: 05.55.22N, 102.45.30E

Average depth: 13 m

Maximum depth: 25 m

Dive rating:

Photo rating: 3, Macro

Unique features: Boulders, overhangs, caves, pelagic species, reef fish

Hazards: Generally none

Pasir Tani (Shipwreck)

Location: Southwest corner of Pulau Perhentian Kecil

Average depth: 22 m

Maximum depth: 25 m

Dive rating:

Photo rating: 3, Macro

Unique features: Soft and black corals, pelagic species, reef fish

Hazards: Slight surface currents; visibility is marginal

This wreck consists of half a steel landing craft used by Vietnamese boat people seeking refuge in Malaysia. Although not a particularly attractive wreck, it has become a habitat for a diverse range of marine life. Sizeable soft coral trees (*Dendronephthya*), black corals and ever-present colourful featherstars act as a playground for a dazzling multitude of reef fish species including hawkfish, angelfish, batfish, barracudas, snappers, wrasses, jacks, groupers and stingrays. You may want to be the first one at the wreck as visibility becomes rather poor with more than half a dozen divers stirring up the sandy bottom.

Tanjung Besi is a continuation of Pulau Perhentian Besar's rocky coastline. Submerged rocks and boulders set through by caves and overhangs make for a visually interesting dive. The surfaces of the granite boulders are topped with prolific featherstars, soft corals, gorgonian fans and large sea fans. You might want to explore the sandy bottom away from the boulders to see scorpionfish, blue-spotted stingrays, damselfish, gobies, star puffers, lizardfish and occasional resting white-tip sharks and nurse sharks. Patches of bubble corals containing symbiotic shrimps and anemones and the lovable, but sometimes combative, clownfish share this site with moray eels, sea stars and sea urchins. Besides shoals of snappers, yellowtail barracudas, jacks, fusiliers, giant groupers, wrasses and sweetlips, pelagic species frequent this area due to the exposure to the open sea to the north.

For divers with a little patience and the propensity to observe macro life, it is worthwhile dedicating an entire dive exploring the overhangs and caves. Closer inspection will reveal a variety of life forms such as cleaner shrimps and nudibranchs among the encrusting corals and rocks.

Other notable dive sites

Pulau Serenggeh (depth 13–20 metres) is located 200 metres south of Tokong Laut. The site consists of a jumble of rocks with nice soft coral coverage and sightings of kingfish, nudibranchs and bamboo sharks.

Pulau Susu Dara Besar (north side) and **Pulau Susu Dara Kecil** (north side), about 200 metres northeast of Tokong Laut, have many features in common with nearby Tokong Laut although the coral coverage is not as prolific. Both sites are at a depth of 12–18 metres.

Teluk Kerma (depth 10–18 metres), at the northwestern tip of Pulau Perhentian Kecil, has a good variety of hard coral and a diverse population of pufferfish, bumphead parrotfish, snappers and stingrays.

Batu Nisan (depth 8–15 metres), at the eastern tip of Pasir Panjang, is an easy dive among patches of hard corals that extend to the sandy bottom where stingrays, turtles and nudibranchs are common sights.

Right: Teira batfish (*Platax teira*) occasionally 'adopt' divers, curiously accompanying them during a dive.

PULAU
LANG TENGAH

Coordinates: 05.47N, 102.53E

Left: Sea anemone and *Acropora*

Inset: A hingebeak shrimp (*Rhynchocinetes*) in close 'contact' with sea urchins (*Diadema savignyi*)

Located between the Perhentian islands and Pulau Redang is the small island of Pulau Lang Tengah (Middle Eagle Island), which derived its name from the once healthy eagle population nesting on the island. It is a very underrated dive destination that has the potential to become as popular as its neighbouring islands.

The clear emerald waters and the coral-fringing reefs surrounding the island have attractions for scuba divers and snorkellers alike. The island itself is covered by hilly tropical rainforest that offers varied flora and fauna for those willing to trek across the island.

Diving Pulau Lang Tengah

The dive sites of Pulau Lang Tengah are found mostly on the southwestern fringes of the island. Although it has been decimated by excessive development, boat traffic and snorkelling, the shallow house reef in front of Square Point Resort still retains some coral cover (mainly staghorn coral) and provides opportunities to spot adult black-tip reef sharks that frequent the shallow areas of the reef. There is a clear reef edge which is marked by surface buoys. Here, the bottom slopes away quickly into deeper blue waters. The resorts on the island operate dive centres that organise dives in the surrounding waters as well as day trips to Pulau Redang.

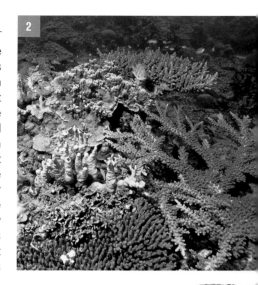

1 & 2: Expanses of table coral (*Acropora hyacinthus*)

3: Juvenile yellow-margined moray eels (*Gymnothorax flavimarginatus*)

Getting There

Pulau Lang Tengah can be reached via Kuala Terengganu. Both Malaysia Airlines (www.malaysiaairlines.com) and AirAsia (www.airasia.com) operate daily flights there. The transfer from Sultan Mahmud Airport to the coastal village of Tanjung Merang takes about 30 minutes.

If you are driving, make your way to Kuala Terengganu via the east coast highway and then proceed to Tanjung Merang. Ample secure parking is available at the ferry terminal at a reasonable rate. Alternatively, air-conditioned coaches operated by Transnasional travel daily to Kuala Terangganu. The transfer to Tanjung Merang takes about 30 minutes.

The boat/ferry services to Pulau Lang Tengah depart from Tanjung Merang Jetty and are operated by the resorts. They typically depart in the morning and return at noon. The transfer takes about 40 minutes.

Accommodation

Blue Coral Island Resort
Pulau Lang Tengah, Terengganu
Tel: (60) 9 356 914 / (60) 3 705 2577
Fax: (60) 9 238 0910 / (60) 3 705 2579
Email: maxcarry@tm.net.my
Website: www.malaysiaislandresorts.com

Square Point Resort
Kuala Terengganu Office: 200 & 202 Jalan Bandar
20100 Kuala Terengganu, Terengganu
Tel: (60) 9 623 5333 / (60) 9 623 7763
Fax: (60) 9 623 9533
Email: sale@langisland.com
Website: www.squarepointresort.com

Redang Lang Island Resort
Kuala Terengganu Office: 1129, 1st Floor, Jalan Bukit Kecil
21100 Kuala Terengganu, Terengganu
Tel: (60) 9 623 9911
Fax: (60) 9 631 0832
Email: boon@redanglangresort.com.my
Website: www.redanglangresort.com.my/

D'Coconut Lagoon
Pulau Lang Tengah, Terengganu
Tel: (60) 3 4252 6686 / (60) 3 4256 5753 / (60) 3 4291 1808
Fax: (60) 3 4252 2689
Email: dcoconut@tm.net.my / dcoconut@dcoconutlagoon.com
Website: www.dcoconutlagoon.com

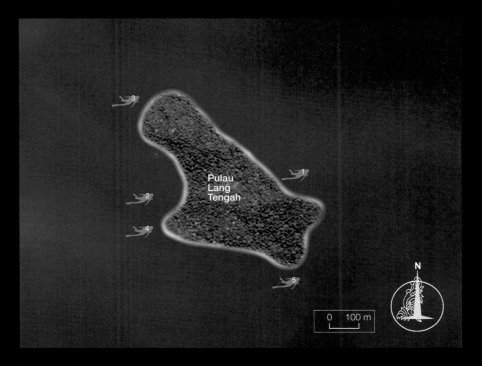

Key for Dive Sites

1: Batu Bulan   4: Batu Kuching
2: Batu Nayak Keras   5: Terumbu Kuning
3: Karang Nibong Laut

Batu Bulan

Location: 05.47.33N, 102.54.11E

Average depth: 8 m

Maximum depth: 12 m

Dive rating:

Photo rating: 2, Wide angle

Unique features: Sandy bottom with boulders, staghorn coral, table coral

Hazards: None

If you descend just north of Square Point Resort and maintain a northerly direction, you will come across Batu Bulan, a very shallow dive in an almost surreal seascape. When visibility is good, it feels as though you are diving in an aquarium. The sandy seafloor, almost powdery in its composition, is interspersed with rock boulders and stacks of staghorn and table corals. Split-banded cardinalfish, butterflyfish and damselfish dart around the coral structures, providing a very colourful contrast. The seabed is home to sea cucumbers and goatfish, forever sifting the sand for organic, edible material.

Batu Nayak Keras

Location: 05.47.20N, 102.52.25E

Average depth: 16 m

Maximum depth: 22 m

Dive rating:

Photo rating: 3, Macro

Unique features: Cleaner shrimps, symbiotic shrimps, razorfish, moray eels

Hazards: None

Descending initially to around 20 metres, you will reach a boulder-strewn seabed with occasional patches of acroporus and sponges as well as small schools of reef fish like yellowtail snappers and fusiliers. However, the macro life forms make up the more interesting aspects of this site. Cleaner and other species of symbiotic shrimps live on many of the corals, boulder outcrops and starfishes. Ascending to the shallower area of the reef slope, boulders festooned with tube worms and featherstars shelter undulated moray eels. Occasionally, three or four share a crevice or small cave and curiously investigate anything that passes by.

Below: Grape-like bubble corals (*Plerogyra*) are water-filled vesicles that protect the delicate inner polyps.

Karang Nibong Laut

Location: Northwestern tip of the island

Average depth: 18 m

Maximum depth: 24 m

Dive rating:

Photo rating: 3, Wide angle

Unique features: Turtles, pelagic species including jacks and barracudas

Hazards: Some surface currents

As this site is swept by tidal currents, it frequently attracts pelagic species such as barracudas, jacks and, during the earlier part of the season, a whale shark. The corals are home to wrasses, rabbitfish, butterflyfish, green turtles and hawksbill turtles.

Other notable dive sites

Batu Kuching (depth 20 metres) is located on the southwestern edge of the island. The site consists of a boulder arrangement that resembles a cat. Sea whips, barrel sponges and hard corals are home to glass sweepers, wrasses, butterflyfish and snappers.

Terumbu Kuning (depth 20 metres) is on the southern tip of Pulau Lang Tengah. It is characterised by rock structures that slope to the sandy bottom. Groupers, barramundi cod, nurse sharks, batfish, jacks and fusiliers are present.

BIDONG
ARCHIPELAGO

Coordinates: 05.40.2N, 103.02.3E

Left: An extraordinarily rich panorama of reef fish surrounding a hard coral (*Tubastrea micrantha*)

Inset: This shallow reef is full of life and colours.

Six islands and some outcrops with fringing reefs make up the Bidong group of islands. The islands are 22 kilometres from Pulau Redang and 24 kilometres from Kuala Terengganu, the state capital of Terengganu. Pulau Bidong was declared a UN refugee camp for Vietnamese boat people fleeing their war-torn homeland. As a result, no visitors were allowed on or around the island. Although the access restrictions have now been lifted, few divers venture here despite its proximity to popular Pulau Redang, probably due to logistical and infrastructural constraints placed on the local operators.

Diving Bidong Archipelago

Being off the beaten track of mainstream diving on the east coast of the peninsula, the reefs around Bidong Archipelago are largely undisturbed and, as is the case with Pulau Tenggol, the distance from the mainland makes for a prolific marine ecosystem.

Surface conditions are best between April and May. Visibility is best in April and at the beginning of October. Average visibility is 15 metres. Due to some thermoclines in July, visibility can drop to only a few metres. During this time, diving should be limited to the shallower reefs where visibility remains good.

Hard corals prevail in the shallow areas of the fringing reef slopes while gorgonians, sea fans and black coral are found in the deeper waters. Soft corals are also abundant. Pelagic species like jacks, barracudas and sharks frequent the open waters off the reef slopes.

1: A school of chevron barracudas (*Sphyraena putnamiae*) frequenting a stretch of reef swept by strong currents

2: Batfish (*Platax teira*), a species always appreciated by underwater photographers

Getting There and Accommodation

A live-on-board safari is the most sensible way to explore the reefs around Bidong Archipelago as no permanent dive operators have set up on the islands to date. Alternatively, check with the dive operators on Pulau Redang for day trips.

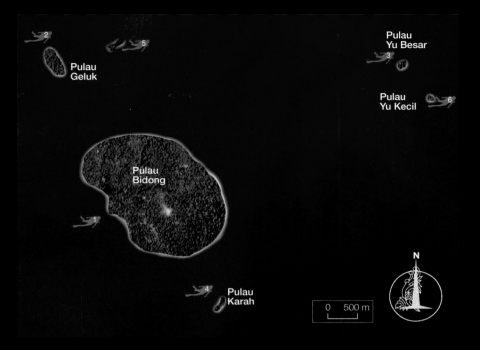

Key for Dive Sites

1: Bidong Bay	3: Pulau Yu Besar (Big Shark Island)	5: Batu Takorak
2: Pulau Geluk	4: Karah Reef	6: Pulau Yu Kecil

Bidong Bay

Location: Fronting the western edge of Pulau Bidong

Average depth: 10 m

Maximum depth: 15 m

Dive rating: 🤿 🤿 🤿

Photo rating: 3, Macro

Unique features: Lionfish, moray eels, stonefish, a host of macro life

Hazards: None

This site is reminiscent of a shipyard as it is dominated by boats sunk by the arriving Vietnamese that have now become artificial reefs. Extensively covered with soft and encrusting corals, the wrecks are home to moray eels, stingrays and a variety of small fish. The decks are populated by a plethora of graceful flatworms, colourful nudibranchs and crustaceans.

Below: A reef slope decorated with lush soft corals (*Siphonogorgia* sp.) and sponges (*Jaspis stellifera*)

Facing page: An elegant colony of Dendrophyllia (*Tubastrea micrantha*)

Pulau Geluk

Location: Off the northern tip of Pulau Bidong

Average depth: 15 m

Maximum depth: 20 m

Dive rating:

Photo rating: 3, Macro

Unique features: Pelagic species, shoals of trevallies, snappers, wrasses

Hazards: None

The seascape surrounding Pulau Bidong, especially at the northern end, is made up of rocks and boulders which extend to the sandy bottom at around 20 metres. Shoals of trevallies, snappers and yellowtail fusiliers are ever present as are rainbow runners, kingfish, barracudas, spotted rays and different types of angelfish, butterflyfish and wrasses. The boulders and rocks on the sandy patches are home to colourful Christmas tree worms, sea stars, lizardfish, pufferfish and sea cucumbers.

Pulau Yu Besar
(Big Shark Island)

Location: Off the northern tip of Pulau Bidong

Average depth: 18 m

Maximum depth: 24 m

Dive rating:

Photo rating: 3, Macro

Unique features: Pelagic species, shoals of trevallies, snappers, wrasses

Hazards: None

The rugged terrain of this site descends to a colourful coral garden interspersed with bubble corals, acroporus, soft corals, sponges and featherstars. Given the open sea currents sweeping through this area, it is home to a rich diversity of reef fish including schooling yellowtail fusiliers, barracudas, trevallies, rainbow runners, batfish and a number of giant humphead parrotfish. This area was once teeming with white-tip and black-tip reef sharks, hence the island's name, but such sightings are now rare.

Karah Reef

Location: Between the southern tips of Pulau Bidong and Pulau Karah

Average depth: 18 m

Maximum depth: 30 m

Dive rating:

Photo rating: 3, Macro

Unique features: Boulders with rich growth of soft corals, crustaceans, pelagic species

Hazards: Persistent currents

Above: Black-spotted porcupinefish (*Diodon hystrix*) are able to inflate themselves and project outward-pointing spines to deter predators.

Facing page: Scores of holothurians (*Synaptula* sp.) feeding on the substances secreted by barrel sponges (*Xestospongia testudinaria*)

The channel between Pulau Bidong and Pulau Karah experiences currents that carry nutrients to the reef. The large granite boulders on the seabed are covered with colourful soft corals, featherstars, sponges and tube worms, all of which are home to a multitude of crustaceans and invertebrates. Common encounters include jacks, clown triggerfish, barracudas and the occasional shark. It is advisable to head into the current and finish off drifting to the exit point.

Other notable dive sites

Batu Takorak (depth 20–25 metres) is located north of Pulau Bidong. It is home to pelagic species such as barracudas and jacks and also has a healthy growth of coral.

Pulau Yu Kecil is surrounded by deeper waters and is home to barracudas, mackerel, bumphead parrotfish and sharks.

PULAU KAPAS
& PULAU GEMIA

Coordinates: 05.31.30N, 103.39.0E

Left: Red whip coral (*Junceella* sp.) surrounded by a dense school of nose-spot cardinalfish (*Rhabdamia cypselura*)

Inset: The extraordinary variety and colours of soft corals (*Siphonogorgia* sp.) and gorgonians (*Acanthogorgiidae*)

Pulau Kapas and Pulau Gemia (just north of Pulau Kapas) are about 6 and 8 kilometres respectively from the mainland coastal village of Marang. The islands are surrounded by fringing reefs and generally shallow waters that have a good coverage of acroporus, varieties of soft coral and reef fish. The close proximity of the islands to the mainland makes them a popular destination for day excursions and overnight stays for those seeking a quick getaway.

Diving in Malaysia

Diving Pulau Kapas and Pulau Gemia

Diving around Pulau Kapas and Pulau Gemia is generally in shallow waters (between 8 and 12 metres), allowing long bottom times. Visibility varies from 5 to 15 metres. The marine life around the islands is abundant and includes batfish, eels, blue-spotted stingrays, boxfish and nudibranchs. Pelagic species like jacks, groupers and black-tip and white-tip reef sharks can be found at the deeper regions off the southern fringes of Pulau Kapas due to the exposure to the currents of the South China Sea. Mantas, whale sharks and dolphins can often be spotted at the beginning and end of the diving season.

The eastern side of both islands can experience stronger currents and choppy conditions due to the exposure to the open sea so may make diving challenging to the novice diver. The eastern corners of the islands provide good snorkelling sites that have a healthy variety of coral and reef fish.

Both: A large school of yellow-band fusiliers (*Pterocaesio chrysozona*) patrolling the slopes of the reef

Getting There

Pulau Kapas and Pulau Gemia can be reached via Kuala Terengganu. Both Malaysia Airlines (www.malaysiaairlines.com) and AirAsia (www.airasia.com) operate daily flights there. From Sultan Mahmud Airport, transfer to the coastal village of Marang, which is about 17 kilometres away.

If you are driving, make your way to Kuala Terengganu via the east coast highway and then proceed south to Marang. The car park is located in the jetty area of the village. Alternatively, air-conditioned coaches operated by Transnasional travel daily to Kuala Terengganu. Then transfer to Marang.

Depending on the type of boat you take, the ride can last from 10 (speedboat) to 35 minutes (slow boat).

Accommodation

On Pulau Kapas, there are a number of small resorts with basic amenities that are located, more or less, next door to one another. The island also has some camp sites. On Pulau Gemia, accommodation is very limited. It is confined to some camp sites and one resort.

ON PULAU KAPAS
Kapas Garden Resort
Tel: (6) 011 987 1305
Email: kapasgarden@hotmail.com

Kapas Island Resort
Tel: (60) 9 617 1331/ (60) 9 617 1332
Fax: (60) 9 617 1578

Tuty Puri Island Resort
Tel: (60) 9 624 6090
Fax: (60) 3 716 6916

Mak Cik Gemuk Beach Resort
Tel: (60) 9 624 5120
Fax: (60) 9 618 1221

Zaki Beach Resort
Tel: (6) 019 956 0513

Beauty Island Resort
Tel: (60) 9 624 5088/ (60) 3 421 8528
Fax: (60) 3 422 8228

ON PULAU GEMIA
Gem Island Resort
Pulau Gemia
Marang, Terengganu
Tel: (60) 9 624 5110
Fax: (60) 9 624 5109
Website: www.gemresorts.com

Pulau Gemia

Pulau Kapas

N

0   100 m

Key for Dive Sites

1: Batu Berakit

2: Teluk Lubang

3: Pulau Gemia

4: Coral Garden

5: Japanese Wreck

Batu Berakit

Location: Eastern side of Pulau Kapas

Average depth: 15 m

Maximum depth: 20 m

Dive rating: 🦅 🦅 🦅

Photo rating: 3, Wide angle; 3, Macro

Unique features: Rugged boulders, soft corals, sponges, jacks, snappers, wrasses

Hazards: Occasional stronger currents and waves

Descending to the sandy seafloor at about 20 metres, this site is made up of two large, rugged boulders. The site has a good cover of colourful soft corals, sponges and featherstars and is home to a number of reef fish species including damsels, wrasses, blennies and gobies as well as schools of snappers, bannerfish, fusiliers, parrotfish and Moorish idol fish. If you have a look under the boulder overhangs, you might see some resting bamboo sharks. Macro life consists mainly of corals, cleaner shrimps and the occasional nudibranch.

1: Translucent ascidians (*Rhopalaea crassa*)

2: The reclusive decorator crab (*Camposcia retusa*)

3: The blue-spotted fantail ray (*Taeniura lymna*), the most common type of ray found on coral reefs

4: A spot-face moray (*Gymnothorax fimbriatus*) curiously peeking from its lair

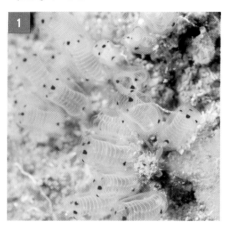

Teluk Lubang

Location: Eastern side of Pulau Kapas

Average depth: 15 m

Maximum depth: 20 m

Dive rating:

Photo rating: 3, Wide angle; 3, Macro

Unique features: Boulders, tunnels, soft corals, sponges, variety of reef fish, stingrays

Hazards: Occasional stronger currents and waves

Located on the eastern side of Pulau Kapas which faces the open sea, this site should definitely be explored. If you dive in a southerly direction, large boulders, tunnels and gaps predominate. If you head north, a plethora of hard and soft corals abound. The site also boasts an underwater tunnel that is a couple of metres long. The rocks on the sandy patches are home to colourful

Christmas tree worms, sea stars, lizardfish, pufferfish, occasional blue-spotted ribbontail stingrays, gobies and sea cucumbers. The northern side of the reef is covered by a variety of coral, including staghorn, table, soft and whip corals, as well as featherstars and barrel sponges.

4

Pulau Gemia

Location: North of Pulau Kapas

Average depth: 8 m

Maximum depth: 15 m

Dive rating:

Photo rating: 2, Wide angle

Unique features: Hard and soft corals, parrotfish, damsels

Hazards: None

This is a shallow dive to a seabed carpeted with hard corals. Acroporus corals dominate the shallower part of the reef while small boulders and rocks with soft corals and featherstars cover the deeper end. Schools of rabbitfish, diamond fish, yellowtail snappers, chromis, damsels, wrasses and parrotfish flit among the coral branches. Occasionally, a school of bumphead wrasses graze through the coral rubble on the seafloor foraging for food.

Japanese Wreck

Location: North of Pulau Kapas

Average depth: 20 m

Maximum depth: 25 m

Dive rating:

Photo rating: 3, Wide angle; 3, Macro

Unique features: Encrusting and soft corals, shoals of reef fish, lionfish, nudibranchs, sharks, stingrays

Hazards: Exceeding bottom time

A boat ride lasting about 30 minutes to the north of Kapas Garden Resort will bring you to the wreck of a Japanese landing craft used during World War II. The descent to the site is with the aid of an anchor line. The wreck is resting upright at a depth of 20 to 25 metres. Sections of the metal hull and anti-aircraft guns are covered with hard and encrusting corals, carpet-like soft corals, featherstars, sea whips and stinging hydroids. Yellowback snappers, fusiliers and batfish loiter around the structure. The interior of the wreck has become home to lionfish, pipefish, eels, damselfish, gobies, cardinalfish and nudibranchs. Moving away from the wreck, you might catch a glimpse of white-tip reef sharks, rainbow runners and the occasional stingray.

1: Green turtles (*Chelonia mydas*) have survived for over 100 million years but are now threatened by human activities.

2: The slopes of the reefs around Pulau Kapas act as playgrounds for schools of yellow-band fusiliers (*Pterocaesio chrysozona*).

3: A clown anemonefish (*Amphiprion percula*)

3

Coral Garden

Location: Northwestern fringe of Pulau Kapas

Average depth: 6 m

Maximum depth: 13 m

Dive rating:

Photo rating: 2, Wide angle; 2, Macro

Unique features: Turtles, humphead parrotfish, barracudas, crustaceans

Hazards: None

This easy, shallow dive in a horseshoe-shaped coral structure slopes to around 13 metres. Located just off the beach, it is a good vantage point to observe green turtles, barracudas and humphead parrotfish. While the corals are rather mediocre, it is worth exploring the gaps and crevices for crustaceans and juvenile reef fish.

PULAU TENGGOL

Coordinates: 04.48.32.N, 103.40.50E

Left: Abundant featherstars (*Comaster multifidus*) cling to the reef base and filter food from the passing current.

Inset: Pulau Tenggol is famed for its multitude of nudibranch species such as *Risbecia tryoni*.

Six islands form Tenggol Archipelago: Pulau Nyireh, Tokong Burung, Tokong Talang, Tokong Laut, Tokong Timur and Pulau Tenggol, which is the largest and only inhabited island. The underwater topography of the island group varies from shallow reefs to deep rocky outcrops and sea mounts. Extensions of the islands' terrain beneath the surface of the surrounding waters, all richly covered with coral life, create dramatic visual effects.

Due to its distance from the mainland, Pulau Tenggol is rewarded with clear, nutrient-rich waters from the South China Sea, which account for the diversity of marine life. The island is made up of sedimentary rock formations and is covered by thick vegetation consisting of tropical rainforest and palm trees. Rich fauna and mammal life from monkeys to large iguanas accentuate the unspoilt nature of the island. The only usable beach is at Teluk Air Tawar, which is where the dive resorts are located. Pulau Tenggol is protected by marine park status.

Diving Pulau Tenggol

Almost forgotten and mostly bypassed by the Malaysian mainstream dive community who frequent Pulau Redang and Pulau Perhentian, Pulau Tenggol is considered one of the best diving sites of Peninsular Malaysia by 'old timers' and the more discerning divers. The best time to dive here is between April and August when the waters are clear and visibility is in excess of 20 metres. The whale shark season is normally from August to October.

Although diving is an exciting affair in Pulau Tenggol, it can be challenging to the novice diver at times as rather fierce currents can sweep the much sought-after sites of Tokong Timor, Tokong Laut and Pulau Nyireh.

You are advised to stay well clear of the beach, especially at dusk, as sandflies make it their calling to pester the unwary. On my last trip, I counted approximately 80 bites on my back, the resulting itch making for a few sleepless nights.

1: A colony of soft corals (*Sinularia* sp.) and featherstars (*Comaster multifidus*) in a picturesque arrangement

2: Lush soft coral (*Dendronephthya* sp.)

3: A close-up of a gorgonian fan (*Melitaheidae*) with extended flower-like feeding polyps

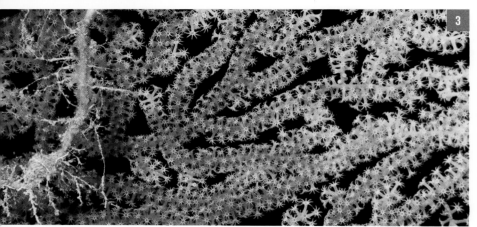

Getting There

Malaysia Airlines (www.malaysiaairlines.com) and AirAsia (www.airasia.com) offer regular daily flights from Kuala Lumpur to Sultan Mahmud Airport in Kuala Terengganu. It is then a 90-minute drive to Dungun, the departure point to Pulau Tenggol. Alternatively, you can take a flight from Kuala Lumpur to Kuantan, which is 1 hour and 40 minutes by taxi or car from Dungun. It is advisable to get an early morning flight as the transfer boat normally leaves at 10 am.

Kuala Terengganu is the main hub for express buses and coaches travelling in and out of the state. Long-distance taxis are also readily available and can take passengers as far as Kuala Lumpur, Ipoh and Johor Bahru. All these coaches and taxis pass through the main trunk road to Kuala Terengganu via Dungun.

Dungun is a buzzing fishing port. Navigating the river mouth is only possible during high tide and getting the timing wrong may mean waiting a few hours or transferring to the dive boat via a small water taxi. The journey to Pulau Tenggol takes about 1 hour.

Accommodation

Accommodation on Pulau Tenggol ranges from the very basic dormitory-style wooden A-frame huts to comfortable, private individual chalets with air-conditioning.

Tenggol Island Resort
Main Office: 210 Jalan Yahaya Ahmad
23000 Kuala Dungun, Terengganu
Tel: (60) 9 848 4862
Fax: (60) 9 845 7302
Email: tenggol@tm.net.my
Website: www.tenggolisland.com

Aimers Island Resort
Main Office: 8 Taman Sutera Kampung Sura
23000 Kuala Dungun, Terengganu
Tel: (60) 9 845 7578

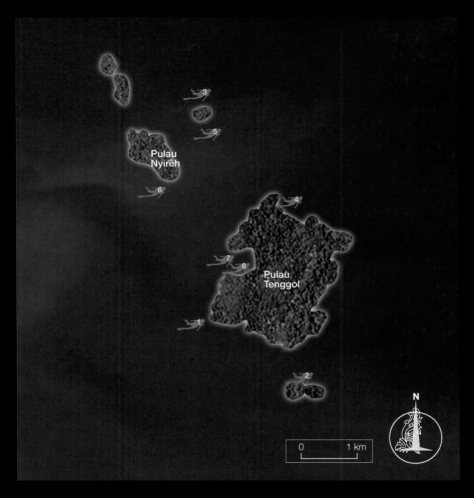

Key for Dive Sites

1: Tanjung Gemok

2: Tokong Timur

3: Tokong Laut

4: Rajawali Reef

5: Pulau Nyireh (The Highway)

6: Amazing Grace

7: Teluk Air Tawar (Fresh Water Bay)
   or Turtle Point

8: Five Sisters

Tanjung Gemok

Location: 04.48.30N, 103.40.45E

Average depth: 25 m

Maximum depth: 35 m

Dive rating: 🤿 🤿 🤿

Photo rating: 3, Wide angle

Unique features: Shoals of jacks, fusiliers, parrotfish, gorgonians, whips, green turtle

Hazards: Strong currents; occasional down currents

This site is south of Aimers Island Resort on the southeastern part of the island. Descending with a northerly current to the sandy seafloor at about 35 metres, the current can, at times, be challenging and turn the dive into a rollercoaster ride hurling the diver from rock to rock, punctuated by spurts of strong current. Schools of golden trevallies, yellowtail snappers, fusiliers, big-eye trevallies, gobies with symbiotic shrimps, a school of juvenile parrotfish and a lone green turtle are some of the exciting encounters. Extending their polyps into the nutrient-rich current, a significant number of sea whips, gorgonians and sea fans populate the seabed. A huge sloping boulder ascending to the surface of the sea and completely covered with colourful soft corals provides a dramatic view in the soft light of the late afternoon.

Facing page: Brightly coloured soft coral (*Siphonogorgia*) clinging to the reef slope

1: A cluster of soft corals (*Sarcophyton* and *Dendronephthya*)

2: Reef-building hard corals (*Acropora florida*)

3: Black coral bush (*Antipathes*)

Tokong Timur

Location: 04.48.19N, 103.40.50E

Average depth: 25 m

Maximum depth: 32 m

Dive rating: 🤿 🤿 🤿 🤿

Photo rating: 4, Wide angle

Unique features: Shoals of snappers, barracudas, bannerfish, carpet of soft corals

Hazards: Strong surface currents; can be a challenge to inexperienced divers

A 15-minute boat ride to the south of Telok Air Tawar leads to an assembly of elongated rocks in a roughly east-west direction that barely break the surface of the sea. Entering the water at the southern side, and depending on the time of day, a fast descent is advisable to avoid being washed into the open sea. The surface swell and the current can be strong and you should note that their direction and strength change at different times of the season. Reaching a maximum depth of 32 metres, big boulders and rocky outcrops characterise this site.

Common sights include large schools of snappers, bannerfish, fusiliers, lizardfish barracudas, ever-present parrotfish and Moorish idol fish. Turning the corner to the northern side of Tokong Timur, the dive becomes a more relaxing drift dive. Ascending to the shallower area of the reef, magnificent rock walls covered with a multitude of colourful soft corals and sponges make for a fitting end to this dive.

1: A blenny (*Escenius*) taking refuge in a small hole among the rocks

2: Anemonefish (*Amphirion*) forming a symbiotic relationship with their host

3: A typical boulder formation of Tenggol Archipelago

4: Lush soft coral (*Dendronephthya*)

Tokong Laut

Location: 04.50.52N, 103.40.08E

Average depth: 22 m

Maximum depth: 32 m

Dive rating:

Photo rating: 4, Wide angle

Unique features: Pelagic species, seasonal whale sharks, swim-thrus

Hazards: Strong currents; for experienced divers only

Located to the northeast, Tokong Laut is a clear favourite among regular divers. Schools of pelagic species are regularly encountered, with sightings of whale sharks not uncommon during the later part of the season. The terrain is generally rocky with huge boulders forming walls, canyons and swim-thrus. Underwater photographers get their money's worth due to the diverse range of coral formations growing on the walls of the boulders. Divers may experience strong currents in this area.

Rajawali Reef

Location: 04.49.05N, 103.40.50E

Average depth: 15 m

Maximum depth: 32 m

Dive rating:

Photo rating: 3, Wide angle; 3, Macro

Unique features: Magnificent rock wall and boulders, shoals of fish, nudibranchs

Hazards: None

1: A magnificent sea fan (*Plexauridae*) in full bloom

2: Black corals (*Antipathes* sp.) are normally found in the deeper regions of the reef.

3: Rich coral growth, mainly *Acropora*

The northern side of the island is often neglected due to the exciting dives at Tokong Timur and Tokong Laut. However, the rock walls of Rajawali Reef, which drop vertically to a depth of approximately 32 metres, are a sight to behold.

The bottom is characterised by large boulder formations and a healthy growth of encrusting corals. Drifting along the wall, schools of snappers, barracudas, the occasional black-tip reef shark, stonefish, crocodile fish, playful schools of juvenile batfish and an immense variety of nudibranchs make this dive truly special. This is a very easy and relaxing dive, especially for novices who will enjoy the magnificent seascape, swim-thrus and passages.

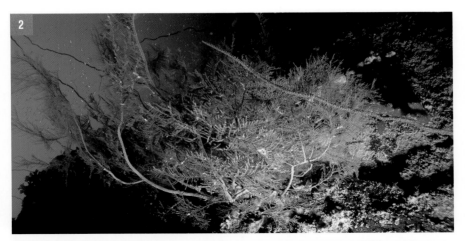

Pulau Nyireh (The Highway)

Location: 04.49.43N, 103.40.43E

Average depth: 22 m

Maximum depth: 35 m

Dive rating: 🤿🤿🤿🤿

Photo rating: 4, Wide angle

Unique features: Pelagic species, seasonal whale sharks, swim-thru

Hazards: Strong currents; for experienced divers only

Pulau Nyireh is a favourite site of many repeat visitors. Also known as the Highway, schools of pelagic fish ply along this 'channel' between Pulau Nyireh and Tokong Laut. The terrain is generally rocky with huge boulders that create walls, tunnels and swim-thrus. Shoals of batfish, yellow-lined barracudas, fusiliers and yellowtail snappers are present in large numbers. The interesting coral formations sprouting on the walls between the boulders covered with gorgonians, sponges, sea fans and soft corals are a photographer's delight. Scores of nudibranchs, sea cucumbers and starfish litter the bottom. You may experience rather strong currents in this area.

Amazing Grace

Location: Southern tip of Pulau Nyireh

Average depth: 28 m

Maximum depth: 38 m

Dive rating: 🤿 🤿 🤿

Photo rating: 3, Wide angle

Unique features: Pelagic species, seasonal whale sharks, swim-thru

Hazards: None

This dive site offers excellent visibility, boasts rich marine life and is only 15 minutes by boat from Teluk Air Tawar. Divers, as well as snorkellers, will enjoy the variety of shoaling fish here. At 2 metres, snorkellers can observe baby sharks while divers will find stunning coral formations intercepted by sandy areas at 15 to 17 metres. Blue-spotted rays, stonefish, scorpionfish and crocodile fish camouflage themselves on the sandy seafloor, waiting for passing prey. A closer inspection of the reef will reveal numerous nudibranchs, the very shy yellow boxfish, juvenile porcupinefish, pufferfish, juvenile white-tip sharks and nurse sharks. Literally tons of gobies and blue-spotted stingrays have made their home here. A large variety of soft corals encrust the large boulders at a progressively shallower depth. Whip corals, sea fans, gorgonians, symbiotic anemone clownfish, damselfish, moray eels, schools of yellowtail snappers and a host of other macro life can also be found.

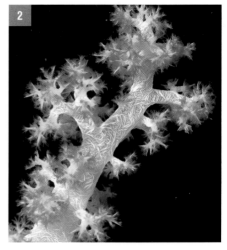

Teluk Air Tawar (Fresh Water Bay) or Turtle Point

Location: 04.48.32N, 103.40.50E

Average depth: 15 m

Maximum depth: 18 m

Dive rating: 🐟 🐟

Photo rating: 3, Wide angle

Unique features: Hard and encrusting corals, lionfish, crustaceans, eels

Hazards: None

To the left of Tenggol Island Resort is a relaxing dive that reaches a depth of 20 metres. It is made up mostly of a sandy seabed, some hard coral, encrusting coral and acroporus. This site is most interesting at the shallower depth of about 5 to 8 metres as a variety of species including resident lionfish, fusiliers, cod and yellow snappers can be found here. Reef fish are not much in evidence in the deeper region.

Upon closer inspection of the boulders and coral formations, you will discover a multitude of habitants: lizardfish lying in wait for unsuspecting prey, tube worms disappearing into crevices at the slightest disturbance and colourful nudibranchs. The frequently encountered crown-of-thorns starfish speaks of the danger to the reef as it is one of the most ferocious predators of healthy corals.

For night dives, this is the site of choice as it comes alive with resident bumphead parrotfish, wrasses, moray eels, bubble shrimps, crabs and a variety of other crustaceans.

Other notable dive sites

There are five wrecks, aptly named the **Five Sisters**, located in the bay. The first is at around 24 metres. The remaining four go down to a depth in excess of 40 metres and are strung like a strand of pearls. Although quite barren in terms of coral growth, the wrecks are home to stonefish, crocodile fish, scorpionfish and nudibranchs. It is very easy to exceed the allowable bottom time while exploring the wrecks so make sure you monitor the dive computer.

1: Variegated lizardfish (*Synodus variegatus*) are efficient reef predators.

2: A close-up of soft coral (*Scleronephthya* sp.)

3: The dense growth of sponges (*Haliclona* sp. and *Cribrochalina olemda*)

4: The breathtaking beauty of soft corals (*Siphonogorgia* sp.)

PULAU TIOMAN

Coordinates: 2°5N, 104°10E

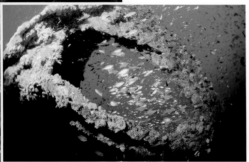

Left: Schooling big-eye trevallies (*Caranx sexfasciatus*)

Inset: Remnants of shipwrecks provide a habitat for a multitude of reef fish species like this school of neon fusiliers (*Pterocaesio tile*).

Pulau Tioman, made famous as the fictitious paradise Bali Hai in the 1960s box office hit musical *South Pacific*, is the largest island on the east coast of Peninsular Malaysia. Located in the South China Sea, it is approximately 32 kilometres from Mersing, the closest mainland port. Measuring 22 kilometres long and 11 kilometres at the widest point, the island has a total land area of 134 square kilometres.

Pulau Tioman is situated in the state of Pahang, the largest state in Peninsular Malaysia. In its early history, Pulau Tioman was known as a stopover for sailors, fishermen and traders. Malay fishermen settled on the island several hundred years ago and there are now six major villages on the island, mainly on the west coast.

Geologically, Pulau Tioman, the largest of a group of 64 volcanic islands, was separated from the mainland only 10,000 years ago, a time when much of Southeast Asia was dry land and sea levels were about 100 metres lower than current depths. Today, the island has a hilly topography and is covered mostly by tropical rainforest. It also has inland forest and narrow flat areas along the coast. Several river systems originating in the hilly, forested areas provide the main supply of fresh water to the island's inhabitants. Small patches of mangrove swamp forests are located on the western part of the island. More than 40 species of mammal, 138 species of bird and 25 species of snake are found on the island, including protected species like the red-giant flying squirrel and the long-tailed macaque.

However, it is the sea and the beaches that attract most visitors, particularly snorkellers and divers, to Pulau Tioman. The reefs around Pulau Tioman and nearby islands have many varieties of coral and tropical reef fish as well as larger species such as turtles and sharks. Aside from diving, snorkelling and canoeing, hardly any other water sports are on offer. For nature-oriented visitors, the interior of the island makes for some very interesting hiking and is rich in fauna, mammals and bird life.

Popular beaches include the ones around the villages of Tekek, Genting, Ayer Batang and Salang. Salang is probably the most sought after by divers due to its close proximity to dive sites, plentiful dive centres, international clientele and buzzing nightlife. Many tourist facilities such as chalets, rest houses, food stalls, jetties and hotels have been built, either by the state government or the private sector. These extensive developments, which have taken place over the last 10 years, have had an adverse impact on the island's environment, especially the marine ecosystem. Some of the fringing reefs and smaller islands (e.g. Pulau Renggis) fronting the resorts have experienced serious degradation and damage to their coral cover and marine life through pollution and human activities.

The marine area surrounding Pulau Tioman and eight nearby islands has been demarcated and gazetted as marine parks and marine reserves. The purpose of the marine parks and reserves is to conserve and protect marine flora and fauna from being destroyed by fishing and other human activities. Although the marine

park status should nominally afford the reefs the necessary protection, self-policing and educating visitors need to be strengthened to preserve this beautiful island and its ecosystem.

Diving Pulau Tioman

Diving activities are usually confined to the west coast of Pulau Tioman, with the best sites located around the northwesterly situated islands of Tulai, Chebeh, Sepoi, Soyak, Labas and Renggis. All these sites are about 10 to 13 kilometres from Salang or Tekek and are reachable within 20 to 30 minutes by boat. The east coast of Pulau Tioman does not have any significant coral growth, with the exception of some encrusting and soft corals, due to its exposure to severe weather and waves during the monsoon season.

Sea conditions from March to October are usually calm and suitable for both diving and snorkelling. Some sites such as Tiger Rock, Pulau Chebeh and Magicienne Rock experience strong surface currents during spring and neap tidal movements, which dissipate as you descend deeper. It is not possible to dive during the northeast monsoon season, which lasts from November to February. Most dive sites have marker buoys to prevent anchor damage. These also serve as descent lines and safety stop aids. Visibility can range from 8 to 20 metres and is usually best from March to May and September to October.

Dive centres and resorts are concentrated on Salang and Tekek beaches. These offer everything from leisure activities to advanced diving and respective training and certification. Dive Asia and the B & J Diving Centre on Salang Beach rent Nitrox and semi-closed rebreather (SCR) and closed circuit rebreather (CCR) facilities and equipment. These, of course, are accessible to suitably qualified customers only. Training required for this type of specialised diving is available. The house reefs serve as training sites and night dive locations. Typically, boat dives to the nearby islands are arranged by the dive centres.

Below: Neon triplefins (*Helcogramma striata*) perched on carpet-like soft coral (*Lobophyton*)

Getting There

Berjaya Air (www.berjaya-air.com) flies direct daily to Pulau Tioman. It provides transport for people staying at Berjaya Tioman Beach Resort but also services those not staying at that particular resort.

If you do not fly to Pulau Tioman, you will have to get to the small coastal town of Mersing on the east coast of the peninsula. From there, you can take either a speedboat, catamaran or ferry to the island. These stop at Genting, Tekek and Salang jetties.

Accommodation

Ranging from very basic to luxurious, accommodation is plentiful and only metres away from the beach.

Berjaya Tioman Beach Resort
PO Box 4
86807 Mersing, Johor
Tel: (60) 9 419 1000
Fax: (60) 9 419 1718
Email: reserv@b-tioman.com
Website: www.berjayaresorts.com/tioman-beach/info.html

Minang Cove Resort
PO Box 74
86807 Mersing, Johor
Tel: (60) 7 799 7372
Email: sales@minangcove.com.my

Panuba Inn Resort
Panuba Bay
Pulau Tioman
86800 Mersing, Pahang
Tel: (60) 7 799 6348 / (6) 013 772 0454 / (6) 013 747 4038
Email: panuba@hotmail.com

Samudra Swiss Cottage
Lot 520, Kampung Tekek
Pulau Tioman
86800 Mersing, Pahang
Tel: (60) 9 419 1642
Email: contact@samudra-swiss-cottage.com
Website: www.samudra-swiss-cottage.com

Bamboo Hill Chalets
Kampung Air Batang
Pulau Tioman
86800 Mersing, Pahang
Tel: (60) 9 419 1339
Fax: (60) 9 419 1326
Email: bamboosu@tm.net.my
Website: www.geocities.com/bamboosu/

Paya Beach Resort
Kampung Paya
Pulau Tioman
86800 Mersing, Pahang
Resort: (60) 7 799 1432
Fax: (60) 7 799 1436
Email: sales@payabeach.com
Website: www.payabeach.com

Salang Sayang Resort
Kampong Salang
Pulau Tioman
86800 Mersing, Pahang
Tel: (60) 9 419 5020 / (60) 9 419 5044
Fax: (60) 9 419 5019
Email: info@salangsayangtioman.com
Website: www.salangsayangtioman.com

Diving in Malaysia

Pulau
Chebeh

4

Pulau
Sepoi

9

6

Pulau
Labas

10

Pulau
Tulai

5

7   8

2

3

13

11

12

Pulau
Tioman

N

0   2 km

1

Key for Dive Sites

1: Tokong Bahara (Bahara Rock)   6: Magicienne Rock   11: Marine Park
2: Pulau Soyak   7: Tiger Rock   12: Pirate Reef
3: Soyak Wrecks   8: Pulau Labas   13: Sawadee Wreck
4: Pulau Chebeh   9: Genting Bay

Tokong Bahara
(Bahara Rock)

Location: 02.39.37N, 104.03.50E

Average depth: 15 m

Maximum depth: 30 m

Dive rating:

Photo rating: 3, Wide angle

Unique features: Gorgonians, black and soft corals, barracudas, angelfish, butterflyfish

Hazards: Can experience strong surface currents

This site is made up of two rock structures rising from the island plateau. It typically experiences surface currents and is clearly marked by a light beacon for maritime traffic. Entry from a boat is away from the rocks that break the surface of the water. If the boat gets too close, you will be pushed into the rocks. At a depth of around 15 to 18 metres, with the reef slope to your left, the seabed, strewn with boulders and rocky outcrops, has a healthy growth of very colourful soft corals ranging from purple to pink *Dendronephthya* to large blue, lemon, and pink gorgonian sea fans with featherstars clinging to their fragile latticework, black corals and huge barrel sponges. The typical population of marine life includes barracudas, angelfish, butterflyfish, humphead wrasses and parrotfish. At the deeper region where the coral growth tapers off into largely sandy patches, stonefish, crocodile fish, nudibranchs, black-tip reef sharks, nurse sharks and blue-spotted ribbontail rays are not uncommon.

Circumventing Tokong Bahara at 5 to 8 metres, the fringing reef is carpeted with soft corals, sponges and large patches of anemone with accompanying clownfish. Juvenile yellowtail barracudas, Moorish idol fish, yellow boxfish and parrotfish can be seen foraging for food. Visibility can range from 5 to 20 metres, depending on sea conditions but should average about 10 metres. This can be a very rewarding dive when the conditions are right.

1: Sand-gobbling synaptid sea cucumbers (*Synapta maculata*) are efficient filter feeders and can exceed 3 metres in length.

2: A polyclad flatworm (*Acanthozoon* sp.)

3: A close-up of a jellyfish (*Thysanostamidae flagellatum*)

4: Yellow-eye pufferfish (*Arothron immaculatus*) are found often in muddy coastal areas.

Pulau Soyak

Location: 02.53.02N, 104.07.01E

Average depth: 15 m

Maximum depth: 22 m

Dive rating:

Photo rating: 3, Wide angle; 3, Macro for night dives

Unique features: Schools of reef fish, crustaceans, black-tip reef sharks, turtles

Hazards: None

Just to the left of Salang Jetty, Pulau Soyak is a small island surrounded by large underwater rocks and boulders with soft, encrusting corals and acroporus. In addition to many tropical reef fish, common sightings include lionfish, large bumphead parrotfish, nudibranchs and turtles. Night dives can be an exciting affair as, due to the Venturi Effect created in the channel by the tides passing between Pulau Tioman and Pulau Soyak, eagle rays and black-tip reef sharks favour this location for their food supply. Lone barracudas, blue-spotted rays, moray eels, lionfish and a host of crustaceans and invertebrates are found among the rocky protrusions, corals and sandy patches. The best depth range is 8 to 15 metres.

Below: Soft coral (*Dendronephthya* sp.)

Right: Featherstars (*Comanthina nobilis*), primarily nocturnal feeders, taking advantage of strong, nutrient-rich currents during the day

Soyak Wrecks

Location: 5 minutes from Salang Jetty

Average depth: 22 m

Maximum depth: 25 m

Dive rating: 🤿 🤿 🤿

Photo rating: 3, Wide angle

Unique features: Schools of reef fish, groupers, stonefish, snappers

Hazards: None

Located on the side facing the mainland, the two wrecks are covered with a wide variety of soft and encrusting corals. Schools of fusiliers, yellowtail kingfish, snappers and trevallies have made the wrecks their home. Lyre-tailed wrasses follow you around and a giant grouper is often sighted as is a black-tip reef shark that circles the wrecks. The gangways and upper decks near the wheelhouse hide perfectly camouflaged stonefish, flatworms and nudibranchs. Common sights are black-spotted pufferfish and porcupinefish darting in and out of the structures' interiors.

1: Shipwrecks often become home to a vast array of marine life, especially encrusting and soft corals.

2: The interior spaces and superstructure of this wreck provide the perfect playground for schools of yellow-band fusiliers (*Pterocaesio chrysozona*).

3: Shipwreck diving is popular among recreational divers.

Pulau Chebeh

Location: 02.55.85N, 104.05.98E

Average depth: 20 m

Maximum depth: 28 m

Dive rating: 🤿 🤿 🤿

Photo rating: 3, Wide angle

Unique features: Boulders, swim-thru, gorgonians, fans, reef fish

Hazards: Titan triggerfish on the lookout for unsuspecting divers

Pulau Chebeh can be dived at either the northeast or southeast corner, depending on sea conditions and the current. The seascape surrounding the island is made up of very large volcanic rocks and boulders which extend to the sandy seabed at around 28 metres. These boulders and rocks create tunnels and passages that are perfect for divers to swim through and around.

1: An assembly of sea squirts (*Polycarpa aurata* and *Didemnum molle*)

2: Nudibranchs (*Chromodoris bullocki* and *Risbecia tryoni*)

3: A serene seascape in the early morning light

The most prominent features, especially at the southeast corner of the island, are the many colourful *Dendronephthya* soft corals, large white gorgonian sea fans and some black coral. Shoals of trevallies, snappers and parrotfish are ever present as are sea anemones and clownfish, large groupers, spotted rays, different types of angelfish, butterflyfish, wrasses and spotted sweetlips. The boulders and rocks on the sandy patches are home to colourful Christmas tree worms, sea stars, lizardfish, pufferfish, scorpionfish, stingrays, gobies and sea cucumbers. Moray eels tuck themselves away in the countless crevices and gaps, peeking out for a quick inspection

of potential prey. There have also been occasional sightings of whale sharks and manta rays during their annual migration (April and October).

The waters around Pulau Chebeh are notorious for resident titan triggerfish. Local dive stories tell of many a diver who has had an encounter with these fish, especially during nesting periods when their territorial behaviour is at its most aggressive. Be aware that intruding into the nesting area might put you into harm's way. I once had to sacrifice a bit of skin and flesh from my knee during one such encounter.

Golden Reef

Location: Between Pulau Sepoi and Tiger Rock

Average depth: 16 m

Maximum depth: 20 m

Dive rating: 🤿 🤿 🤿

Photo rating: 3, Wide angle

Unique features: Colourful gorgonians, sea fans, stingrays, stonefish

Hazards: None

The Golden Reef is an underwater plateau consisting of occasional rocks and covered with large purple, white and beige gorgonians, sponges, sea fans and whips. Predators such as stingrays, stonefish, scorpionfish and lionfish keep a close eye on shoals of butterflyfish, snappers, angelfish and coral groupers. Where the plateau tapers off into the sandy seafloor, sea cucumbers, sea stars and the occasional crown-of-thorns starfish can be spotted. Typical of sites in this area, surface currents and a sometimes choppy sea dissipate as you descend.

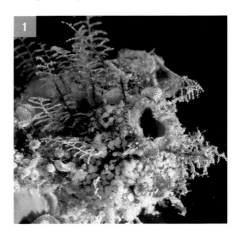

1: Magnificent sea anemones (*Heteractis magnifica*)

2: Encrusting corals and filter feeders, or ascidians

3: Sea fans (*Solenocaulon* sp.) and soft corals
(*Dendronephthya* sp.) decorating the reef slope

4: Encounters with green sea turtles (*Chelonia mydas*) are
not unusual in the waters of Pulau Tioman but are
less frequent than in the past.

Magicienne Rock

Location: 02.54.91N, 104.08.86E

Average depth: 16 m

Maximum depth: 25 m

Dive rating: 🤿 🤿 🤿

Photo rating: 3, Wide angle

Unique features: Pinnacle visited by pelagic species and shoaling reef fish

Hazards: Surface current

This is one dive site that should not be missed. Although the stress on the reef caused either by illegal fishing or excessive human traffic is noticeable, it is still a very exciting location. During spring, tides can be affected by strong surface currents so it is advisable to descend without lingering on the surface.

The rock pinnacle rises to 8 metres below the surface and features hard and encrusting corals and colourful sponges. Due to the strong nutrient-rich current and the pinnacle facing the open sea, pelagic species often congregate here. Seasonal sightings of manta rays, whale sharks and leopard sharks have been reported. Shoals of jacks, golden striped trevallies, snappers, groupers, barracudas, butterflyfish and fusiliers are a common sight.

1: A giant clam (*Tridacna squamosa*) can exceed 1 metre in diameter and can live for up to 200 years.

2: A member of the nudibranch family (*Phyllidia* sp.)

3: Cuttlefish (*Sepia pharaonis*) have the most advanced nervous system of all invertebrates.

4: Soft corals (*Siphonogorgia* sp.)

Tiger Rock

Location: 02.53.46N, 104.03.57E

Average depth: 20 m

Maximum depth: 30 m

Dive rating: 🐋 🐋 🐋 🐋

Photo rating: 3, Wide angle

Unique features: Swim-thru, gorgonians, barracudas, sharks, shoals of reef fish

Hazards: Strong surface currents; best dived during slack tide

Located in the channel between Pulau Sepoi and Pulau Labas, Tiger Reef is definitely a highlight of diving around Pulau Tioman. The site is marked with an anchor buoy and dive boats will normally trail lines from the stern and the bow to help divers get to the descent line or return to the boat. During spring tides, dives may sometimes be aborted due to the strong surface current.

Descending with the aid of the descent line to around 18 metres, the dive starts with a dive through a large jumble of volcanic boulders that rise to a depth of 10 metres and open into a canyon-like seascape. Shoals of batfish, yellow-lined

barracudas, fusiliers and yellowtail snappers are present in large numbers. White-tip and black-tip sharks can also be seen occasionally. The walls between the boulders have a rich growth of gorgonians, sponges, sea fans, soft corals and table corals. Scores of nudibranchs, starfish, fan worms and sea cucumbers litter the bottom as do patches of titan triggerfish and sea urchins. Circumventing Tiger Rock, tuna, rainbow runners, parrotfish, pufferfish, angelfish, emperorfish and wrasses make this dive a never-ending discovery of local marine species.

You should try to finish the dive and do your safety stop at the anchor line as the surface currents will sweep you away from the boat, possibly resulting in a long swim back to the boat or being towed from the chase boat. Visibility ranges from 5 to 20 metres but averages 10 to 12 metres.

1: Adult round batfish (*Platax orbicularis*) often pair up.

2: Jenkins whiprays (*Himantura jenkinsii*) are accomplished hunters of crustaceans.

3: Schools of yellow-band fusiliers (*Pterocaesio chrysozona*) patrolling reef slopes in pursuit of zooplankton

Pulau Labas

Location: 02.53.21N, 104.03.59E

Average depth: 15 m

Maximum depth: 24 m

Dive rating:

Photo rating: 3, Wide angle

Unique features: Diverse range of healthy gorgonians and sea fans

Hazards: None

The subsurface structure of Pulau Labas is essentially a group of large volcanic rocks and boulders. Tunnels and canyon-like crevices have created swim-thrus and the odd 'squeeze-thru', both of which are popular with many divers. As the sea is normally calm, mooring buoys are set at the northern and southern sides of the island and visibility can range from 5 to 15 metres.

Green turtles, blue-spotted marble rays and pufferfish can be seen here in addition to many varieties of reef fish. Staghorn and lettuce corals, giant clams, eagle rays, black-tip and white-tip reef sharks, cuttlefish, barramundi cod, emperorfish, soldierfish, snappers and a school of bumphead parrotfish are often sighted, as are numerous angelfish and butterflyfish.

1: Colourful Christmas tree worms (*Spirobranchus giganteus*)

2: Deposited nudibranch eggs in colourful ribbon-like strands

3: Soft corals (*Sinularia* sp.) and red whip coral
(*Ctenocella pectinata*)

4: The intricate structure of a sea fan
(*Anthothelidae Solenocaulon* sp.)

5: A tube worm (*Sabellastarte* sp.) spreading its feathers

Genting Bay

Location: 02.54.52N, 104.06.04E

Average depth: 15 m

Maximum depth: 30 m

Dive rating: 🐸 🐸 🐸

Photo rating: 3, Wide angle

Unique features: Boulder and rock formations, healthy gorgonians and fans

Hazards: None

Genting Bay slopes away from the northwestern side of Pulau Tulai, levelling off at the sandy seabed at a depth of around 30 metres. The site is characterised by large rock and boulder formations covered by a variety of corals, including white and blue gorgonians, sea fans, black coral, staghorn, large pristine table corals and soft and whip corals. A number of swim-thrus adds to the attraction of exploring the seascape.

Common marine life includes bumphead parrotfish, giant groupers, angelfish, butterflyfish, featherstars, wrasses and lionfish. The sandy bottom is populated with sea cucumbers, sea stars and cushion stars while lizardfish and gobies dart from rock to rock in search of food. As is common in the waters around Pulau Tioman, there are slight surface currents and visibility can range from 6 to 15 metres.

1: The intricate design of soft coral (*Scleronephthya* sp.)

2: Synaptidae (*Euapta godeffroyi*), sand-gobbling bottom feeders

3: A mysterious split boulder

4: Majestic table coral (*Acropora latistella*)

Malang Rock

Location: 02.54.37N, 104.06.48E

Average depth: 13 m

Maximum depth: 18 m

Dive rating: 🐟 🐟 🐟

Photo rating: 3, Wide angle

Unique features: Corals, reef fish

Hazards: None

Malang Rock is a relatively shallow site so it is also a favourite spot for snorkellers. It has two contrasting environments: sheltered and shallow (around 8 metres) on the side facing Pulau Tulai and deeper waters on the other side. The sheltered side features a coral reef with large areas of lettuce corals, potato corals, pavona cactus

and sponges. Frequent sightings include shoals of small barracudas, trevallies and yellowtail snappers in addition to many cuttlefish, nudibranchs and anemones with attending clownfish. Care should be taken not to get too close to the fire corals and stinging hydroids.

On the side facing the sea, large rocks with a variety of colourful soft and hard corals extend to the seafloor at about 18 metres. Sharks and blue-spotted ribbontail rays are sometimes seen in the deeper channel. Other species mingling around are triggerfish, wrasses, lionfish and six-banded and blue-ring angelfish. Lizardfish, gobies, sea cucumbers, sea stars and groups of sea urchins populate the sandy area.

Other notable dive sites

Marine Park (300 m northwest of Tekek Jetty) features eight wrecks at varying depths where corals and shoals of fish abound.

Pirate Reef (200 m northeast of Pulau Renggis) is one of two main breeding sites on Pulau Tioman.

Sawadee Wreck (400 m west of Tekek Beach) is often used for deep dive training and has a good range of marine life.

1: Encrusting coral (*Diploastrea heliopora*)

2: Sea anemone (*Heteractis magnifica*)

3: A pink anemonefish (*Amphiprion perideraion*) defending its host

PULAU AUR & PULAU DAYANG

Coordinates: 02. 26. 6N, 104, 31. 4E

Left: The descent!

Inset: A delightful arrangement of Christmas tree worms (*Spirobranchus giganteus*)

Pulau Aur and the neighbouring smaller islands of Pulau Dayang, Pulau Lang and Pulau Pinang are the most notable dive destinations in Johor Marine Park. Pulau Aur and Pulau Dayang are forested, rocky islands with a few isolated coconut plantations. The sandy beaches are fringed by palm trees and large rock boulders, always worthwhile climbing to watch the sunset over the expanse of the deep blue South China Sea.

The waters around these islands are deeper and clearer than around the region's inner coastal islands. In addition, due to the distance from the mainland, sightings of whale sharks, manta rays and other pelagic species are not uncommon.

Diving Pulau Aur
and Pulau Dayang

Diving ranges from rock boulders and submerged reefs to wrecks. The channel between Pulau Aur and Pulau Dayang is rich with coral reefs in relatively shallow waters. You also have a unique opportunity to dive a wreck just off the shores of Pulau Dayang. Pulau Pinang has steep drop-offs that provide shelter to stingrays, groupers, cuttlefish, large schools of barracudas and sometimes manta rays or whale sharks.

The diving operations are conducted very competently and safely. The boatman of the dive boat normally knows all the good dive spots and the best times to go.

Below: Bubble coral (*Plerogyra*), a delicate coral species

Right: A nudibranch (*Notodoris gardineri*)

Getting There

You will have to make your own way to the coastal town of Mersing, the departure point of the ferries to Pulau Aur and Pulau Dayang. The ferries typically depart around midnight. The boat transfer from Mersing to Pulau Aur and Pulau Dayang takes about 4 hours.

Accommodation

As dive trips to Pulau Aur and Pulau Dayang are organised by dive centres, accommodation will be included in the package. The resorts on the islands excel in simplicity and basic amenities. While this may be perfectly acceptable to dive diehards, others may crave for hot water, overhead fans in seating areas and a wider range of soft drinks and beverages. Sleeping quarters are dormitory-style and adequate. Electricity is supplied by generators that are usually switched off from 9 am to 6 pm, which can be quite bothersome.

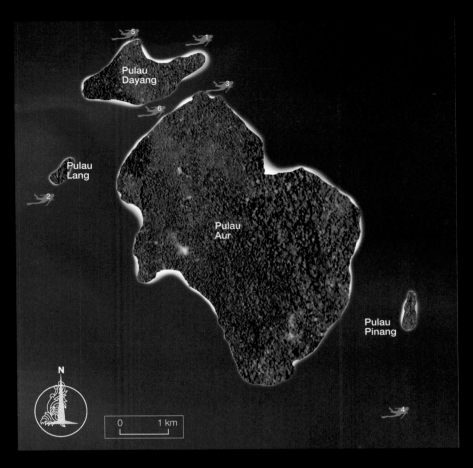

Key for Dive Sites

1: Rayner's Rock   3: Crocodile Rock   5: Captain's Point
2: Pulau Lang   4: Pinnacle   6: Pulau Dayang Jetty

Rayner's Rock

Location: Northwestern tip of Pulau Dayang

Average depth: 15 m

Maximum depth: 40 m

Dive rating: 🦈 🦈 🦈 🦈

Photo rating: 4, Wide angle

Unique features: School of bumphead parrotfish, wrasses, barracudas, prolific macro life

Hazards: Stronger currents away from the rock formation

Probably the most famous and sought-after dive site around Pulau Dayang, Rayner's Rock is a 10-minute boat ride from Dayang Island Resort. The best time to dive the site is early morning, around 7 am. From the surface, it looks like a few rocks and boulders breaking the surface of the sea but this belies the truly magnificent subsurface marine life.

Upon entry into the water and following the descent, the first things you will notice are the excellent visibility, somewhere around 20 to 30 metres, and the deep blue water, prevailing during March to April and September to October. Levelling off at 24 metres, a seabed strewn with hard and soft corals, gorgonian fans and acroporus make for picture-perfect scenery. A school of almost two dozen bumphead parrotfish, unperturbed by snorting and bubbling divers, can normally be seen during early morning dives. Occasionally at the start and end of the

season, you may be able to catch mantas and whale sharks, which come up close to the rock formation at a depth of about 17 to 18 metres. Schools of jacks and barracudas are a common sight if you head away from Rayner's Rock into the open sea. Divers venturing into the open sea should be experienced, carry a compass and be aware of the strong currents.

Upon closer inspection of the boulders and coral formations, you will discover a multitude of inhabitants: lizardfish lying in wait for unsuspecting prey, colourful nudibranchs and tube worms which disappear into crevices at the slightest disturbance and a large variety of reef fish. The frequently encountered crown-of-thorns starfish, being one of the most ferocious predators of healthy corals, speaks of the danger to the reef. Titan triggerfish constantly guarding their nesting area against intruders will make for an interesting photo opportunity, although my buddy had a bite taken out of one of her fins when we got a little too close to the nest—proof that diving with a buddy reduces the statistical probability of a dangerous encounter by 50 per cent.

1: A two-lined monocle bream (*Scolopsis bilineatus*), a common sight in Malaysia's reefs

2: Humphead parrotfish (*Bolbometopon muricatum*) sleep in the same crevice every night.

3: Oriental sweetlips (*Plectorhinchus orientalis*)

1

Pulau Lang

Location: 500 m southwest of Pulau Dayang Jetty

Average depth: 15 m

Maximum depth: 40 m

Dive rating: 🤿 🤿 🤿

Photo rating: 3, Macro

Unique features: Healthy coral growth, acroporus, encrusting coral, sponges, cuttlefish

Hazards: None

Diving in Malaysia

This small island is about 5 minutes away by boat from Pulau Dayang Jetty. The reef slopes away to a depth of about 22 metres, giving way to a densely populated coral system. Predominant species are brain coral, acroporus and gorgonian fans. It is hard to miss the abundant tube worms that reside on the many boulders, however, keep an eye out for nudibranchs which can be spotted along the walls and ledges. Some stress to the reef is evident—extended areas of coral heads have suffered damage as broken fragments litter the seafloor.

This area seems to be a habitat for cuttlefish which can be observed closely and even approached with the right amount of patience. These fish are especially interesting to watch during nesting periods.

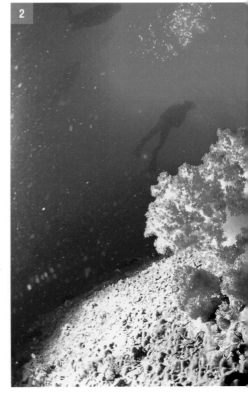

1: A pair of masked rabbitfish (*Siganus puellus*)

2: Soft coral (*Dendronephthya* sp.) and giant clams (*Tridacna maxima*) sharing living space

3: Encrusting coral (*Symphyllia recta*) crowned by hard corals (*Acropora cerealis*)

3

Crocodile Rock

Location: 200 m northwest of Pulau Dayang Jetty

Average depth: 8 m

Maximum depth: 15 m

Dive rating: 🤿 🤿

Photo rating: 3, Macro

Unique features: Boulders, featherstars, juvenile reef fish

Hazards: None

A relatively shallow dive, Crocodile Rock is an ideal site for open water students and snorkellers. The seabed is reminiscent of a white sandy beach with boulders and encrusting corals blanketed with rainbow-coloured tube worms stretching as far as the eye can see. Featherstars in every conceivable colour are abundant and can be found attached to whip coral and boulders swaying with the current. Small shoals of juvenile reef fish dart in and out of the corals with occasional emperorfish and batfish in attendance. Colourful nudibranchs slowly navigate their way over small rocks and hard corals. This site is a good training ground for night dive students although the waters around Pulau Dayang Jetty are home to some very unusual species as well.

1: A two-lined monocle bream (*Scolopsis bilineatus*)

2: An ember parrotfish (*Scarus rubroviolaceus*) settling down for the night

3: A nocturnal swimmer crab (*Thalamita prymna*)

4: A featherstar (*Stephanometra* sp.) clinging to the surface of the reef using appendages called cirri

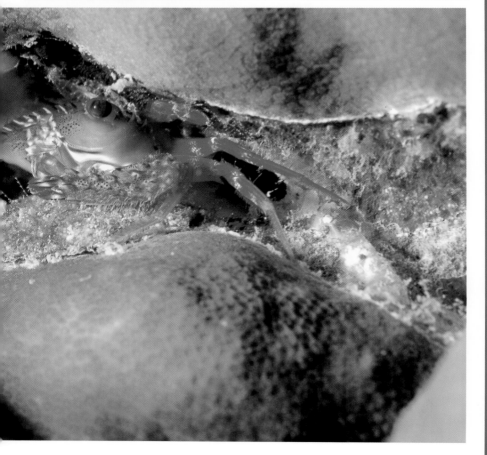

Pinnacle

Location: South of Pulau Aur; 20 minutes by boat and marked by an anchor buoy

Average depth: 22 m

Maximum depth: 30 m

Dive rating:

Photo rating: 3, Wide angle

Unique features: Corals, sponges, moray eels, giant clams, nudibranchs

Hazards: Surface currents can be challenging during entry and exit

Located next to Rayner's Rock, the Pinnacle is one of the highlights of diving Pulau Dayang. The site is made up of a rock formation that reaches 15 metres below the surface. As entry and exit can be challenging due to the strong currents that reach as deep as 8 metres, I recommend you use the anchor buoy line for the descent and safety stop (be careful when grasping the line as microscopic life forms might give you nasty stings or cuts).

At around 15 metres, the Pinnacle slopes away to give way to large boulders and rock formations covered by gorgonians, whips and sea fans in brilliant hues of red. Flower-shaped lettuce coral, sponges, acroporus and table coral are surrounded by shoals of snappers, fusiliers, angelfish and batfish. Moray eels hide in the crevices and caves formed by the jumble of boulders and strikingly coloured giant clams feed in the nutrient-rich current. With a little patience, colourful nudibranchs, flatworms and cleaner shrimps can be discovered among the outcrops.

As at Rayner's Rock, mantas and whale sharks can be sighted at the start and end of the season. You can also see schools of

jacks and barracudas if you head away from the site into the open sea. Circumventing the Pinnacle takes 30 to 40 minutes and bottom time should be monitored.

The site is experiencing some stress and damage caused by overuse and careless divers. It is not unusual to have boatloads of divers congregating at the same time.

1: A garden of hard and soft corals

2: Red whip coral (*Ctenocella pectinata*)

3: Holothurians (*Bohadschia argus*) swaying in the late afternoon currents

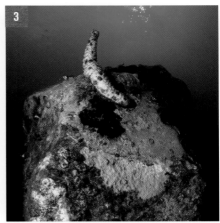

Captain's Point

Location: 02.28.59N, 104.30.56E

Average depth: 15 m

Maximum depth: 30 m

Dive rating:

Photo rating: 3, Macro

Unique features: Coral-covered boulders, variety of reef fish

Hazards: Strong surface currents and drift

Captain's Point is at the most northern point of Pulau Dayang. Due to the prevailing currents, dives can become drift dives in either a southwesterly or northwesterly direction. As there are no anchor buoys, a quick descent is recommended to avoid getting washed onto the rocks. If the current is in your favour, the best direction to head after descending is north of the tip of the island, keeping to the left. Sizeable boulders covered with colourful tube worms, soft corals and featherstars are home to a variety of parrotfish, lizardfish, butterflyfish, snappers and titan triggerfish. Due to the stronger current, pelagic species pass this site in the earlier part of the season.

If you head in the opposite direction, i.e. to the right, all you will see is the occasional boulder in an otherwise barren seascape that slopes into the deep. There are few reef fish although cuttlefish often hover above the few coral patches. If you drift too far to the right, you will surface near Pulau Dayang Jetty.

1: A teira batfish (*Platax teira*)

2: A diver looks at a boulder covered with encrusting coral.

3: Cuttlefish (*Sepia pharaonis*) are very entertaining and photogenic subjects.

Pulau Dayang Jetty (night dive)

Location: Pulau Dayang Jetty

Average depth: 6 m

Maximum depth: 9 m

Dive rating: 🛩 🛩

Photo rating: 3, Macro

Unique features: Featherstars, juvenile stonefish, cleaner shrimps

Hazards: None

As darkness descends upon Pulau Dayang, groups of divers gear up for a night dive. Many groups head out to Pulau Lang and unwittingly miss out on the action taking place right beneath Pulau Dayang Jetty. Therefore, to avoid bumping into divers and bubbles, I recommend the jetty for a short but rewarding night dive.

As you descend to the sandy bottom at about 8 metres, be careful not to stir up the sand and stay close to the pillars supporting the jetty as this is where the marine life congregates. Schools of juvenile yellow snappers dart in and out of the darkness while featherstars clothed in striking red and giant

clams can easily be spotted clinging to the pillars. Nestling in or close to the occasional tyre or discarded construction material are juvenile stonefish which peer curiously at passing divers. Be careful of hydroids which can be mistaken for Christmas tinsel with their luminescent silvery-white branches. Little shrimps and crustaceans reside among the occasional growth of bubble coral but you need to keep an eye out for them or else you will miss them.

2

1: Sea stars (*Fromia monilis*) have astounding regenerating abilities–a completely new animal can grow from a small fragment.

2: Featherstars (*Himerometra robustipinna*) can have as many as 200 arms.

3: Hydroids (*Plumulariidae Gymnagium*) can produce very nasty stings.

4: Crown-of-thorns starfish (*Acanthaster planci*) have sharp toxic spines and should not be handled.

1

PULAU JARAK

Coordinates: 03.58.50N, 100.06.05E

Pulau Jarak lies 70 kilometres west of Lumut or 133 kilometres northeast of Kuala Selangor. It offers an alternative destination for die-hard divers who are unable to frequent their usual east-coast haunts during the northeast monsoon from November to March. The island is a mere rock, uninhabited, overgrown with lush bushes and trees and crowned by a lighthouse. Therefore, the only option for divers is a live-on-board trip.

Left: Bright orange coral (*Tubastrea faulkneri*)–best seen during night dives when its feeding polyps are extended

Inset: A magnificent sea anemone (*Heteractis magnifica*)

Diving Pulau Jarak

Diving Pulau Jarak is a relaxed and fairly easy affair. Due to the small size of the island, it is really one continuous dive site. The only factor you have to consider is whether to dive the eastern or western fringing reef and this depends on the prevailing tidal flow. As the gently sloping reef line extends to a depth of approximately 20 to 25 metres, after which only a sandy bottom is encountered, dives are typically confined to this depth range. As a result, repetitive dives do not pose a problem. In addition, doing 5 or 6 dives a day is not unheard of.

The fact that Pulau Jarak is relatively inaccessible and only dived from November to March seems to provide the reef ecosystem sufficient breathing space to flourish and grow. Visibility during December and January may reach around 10 to 15 metres

Right: The nocturnal sea urchin (*Echinothrix calamaris*) – beware of its spines

Getting There and Accommodation

As there is no accommodation on Pulau Jarak, the only way to get there is by a live-on-board boat. The standard and quality of service on board these boats vary considerably, ranging from cattle-class converted fishing boats to 3-star cruise boats. The best option is to book the *Kaleebso*, one of Malaysia's live-on-board boats. It is a 23-metre vessel that comfortably accommodates up to 20 divers in air-conditioned 2- and 3-bed cabins.

The journey starts in either of the west coast ports of Lumut or Kuala Selangor, depending on where the vessel is anchored. Departure is normally between 7 pm and 11 pm, depending on the prevailing tides on that day. Be advised: If you are late, you might spend about 6 to 8 hours stuck on a sandbank in the river mouth before the incoming tide refloats the vessel to allow it to reach the open sea for the journey to Pulau Jarak.

Diving

in

Malaysia

Pulau
Jarak

N

0   100 m

Key for Dive Sites

1: Whip Garden	4: Moray Harem	7: River Rock
2: North Point	5: East Gardens	8: West Gardens
3: North-South Highway	6: South Point	9: Snapper's Den

Pulau Jarak

Location: 03.58.50N, 100.06.05E

Average depth: 12 m

Maximum depth: 25 m

Dive rating: 🐋 🐋 🐋

Photo rating: 3, Wide angle; 3, Macro

Unique features: Patches of diverse hard and whip corals and sponges, moray eels, anemone clownfish, crustaceans

Hazards: Occasional strong currents

The easterly, or mainland-facing, side of the island makes for easy and relaxed diving as it is protected from the tidal flows of the open sea. Descending to around 15 to 18 metres, the seascape features large, layered hard coral formations. Table top corals, brain corals and tube corals arranged like organ pipes make an excellent habitat for scores of yellowtails, damsels and countless anemone clownfish. Ever-present sea urchins have made their home among most of the coral formations but are not so numerous to become an obstacle to divers as long as you keep your distance. The composition of Pulau Jarak reef does not provide for much soft coral growth, which is limited to a few scattered, richly coloured specimens. You may also encounter moray eels tucked away among the rocky outcrops of the reef, snappers, groupers, lionfish and the occasional green turtle.

The northernmost tip of Pulau Jarak features a stronger running tide, making it a pleasantly relaxed drift dive. If you are lucky, you might be able to meet a lone napoleon wrasse that makes an appearance every now and then.

Night diving around Pulau Jarak reveals a multitude of macro life and crustaceans

that are not visible during the day. They make their presence felt through clicking and crunching noises as they go about feeding. If you shine your dive light onto the reef structure, rich, mesmerising colours spring into view and, with a little bit of patience, shrimps, crabs and cuttlefish appear. Some divers have even claimed to have seen sea horses. Some unusual visitors at night are large sailfish, up to 2 metres long, that curiously explore the boat, bumping against and circling it before disappearing into the night again.

1: A spot-faced moray (*Gymnothorax fimbriatus*) taking a peak at its surroundings

2: Brittle stars (*Ophiothela danae*) weaving an intricate pattern around a coral branch

PULAU LANKAYAN

Coordinates: 06.30.20N, 117.55.18E

Left: Black-tip reef sharks (*Carcharhinus melanopterus*) often enter shallow lagoons in search of food.

Inset: Ringed pipefish (*Doryrhamphus dactyliophorus*) often congregate where sea urchins are present.

Renowned for its excellent marine macro life in a back-to-nature setting, the enchanting island of Lankayan lies 80 kilometres northeast off the coastal city of Sandakan. Pulau Lankayan is part of the Sugud Islands Marine Conservation Area (SIMCA), a private-public sector initiative aimed at protecting and managing the area's marine ecosystem. Since its establishment, SIMCA has produced some encouraging results that have given the ecosystem the opportunity to recover. It has stopped damaging fishing practices such as dynamite and cyanide fishing as well as the excessive development of all the islands within the designated marine zone. Pulau Lankayan is also the destination for green and hawksbill turtles that come ashore to lay their eggs.

While stopping in Sandakan to either catch the boat to Pulau Lankayan or the flight home, a visit to the Sepilok Orang Utan Rehabilitation Centre is highly recommended.

Diving Pulau Lankayan

Given the nature of the seabed, patch and fringing reefs are the norm. As the waters around Pulau Lankayan are part of the continental shelf, the reefs rarely exceed 25 metres, making diving easy and relaxing. Nevertheless, you should not neglect monitoring bottom time. The tidal currents are generally mild and visibility ranges from at least 10 to 15 metres with seasonal variations. Diving is possible throughout the year, although November through December can get wet and windy with the corresponding deterioration of conditions.

Don't miss the daily spectacle of feeding some 30 juvenile black-tip sharks which seem to be conditioned to expect lunch. In barely half a metre of water, the sharks create quite a mêlée. Some even venture onto the sandy beach to grab a morsel, then frantically wriggle back into their natural environment.

The only unpleasant experience is the frequent fish bombs going off in Philippine waters just a few kilometres away. Some of these fish bombs are uncomfortably close, especially when the sea is calm. I dread to think how much destruction is wreaked by this outlawed practice.

1: An emperor shrimp (*Periclimenes imperator*)

2: Flower soft coral (*Xenia*)

3: *Flabellina rubrolineata*, a less common member of the nudibranch family

Getting There

Pulau Lankayan can be reached via the coastal city of Sandakan. Both Malaysia Airlines (www.malaysiaairlines.com) and AirAsia (www.airasia.com) operate daily direct flights from Kuala Lumpur to Sandakan Airport. Alternatively, you can fly to Kota Kinabalu International Airport and then get a connecting flight to Sandakan. Lankayan Island Dive Resort manages the transfer from Sandakan Airport to the boat jetty for onward travel to the island, which takes about 1 hour.

Note: Security measures can be laid to rest as Malaysian Armed Forces personnel are stationed on the island. See also Security and Conservation on pages 194–195.

Accommodation

Lankayan Island Dive Resort
484 Bandar Sabindo
PO Box No 61120
91021 Tawau, Sabah
Tel: (60) 89 765 200
Fax: (60) 89 763 575 / (60) 89 763 563
Email: info@lankayan-island.com
Website: http://lankayan-island.com

Diving in Malaysia

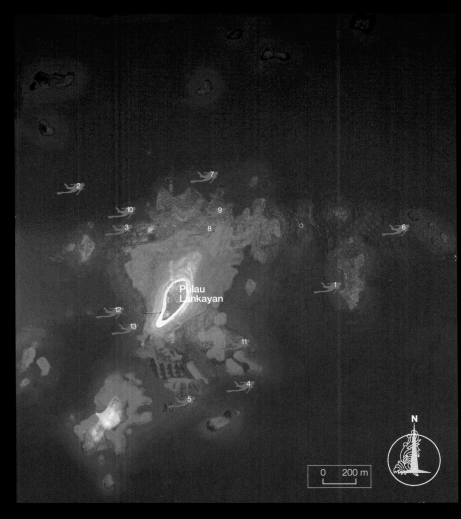

Key for Dive Sites

1: East Reef	6: Mel's Place	11: Mosquito Wreck
2: Sunnu's Lair	7: Reef 77	12: Lankayan Wreck
3: Coral Garden	8: Rock Garden	13: Jetty Wreck
4: Twin Rocks	9: Catching Star	
5: Twin City	10: Veron Fan Garden	

East Reef

Location: Off the eastern side of the island

Average depth: 16 m

Maximum depth: 23 m

Dive rating: *(icons)*

Photo rating: 3, Macro

Unique features: Good coverage of hard and soft corals with an abundance of reef fish

Hazards: None

A short boat ride from the jetty will bring you to East Reef, the largest of the reef structures surrounding Pulau Lankayan. This reef patch is marked by two marker buoys: the larger red buoy at the southern side and the smaller white buoy at the northern end. Descend to about 12 metres, where a colourful, carpet-like expanse of acroporus, lettuce corals, table corals and sponges abounds. The reef tapers off into the sandy bottom at about 22 metres. Bubble corals, small coral crabs, nudibranchs and flatworms populate the edge of the reef. Shoals of yellow snappers, fusiliers, striped catfish, six-banded anglefish, parrotfish, emperorfish, angelfish, soldierfish and cleaner shrimps are present in significant numbers. Even the odd titan triggerfish makes its presence known.

There are still signs of past destructive fishing practices around this reef, including skeletons of acroporus, table corals and pieces of lettuce corals. However, recovery seems to be well under way with plenty of new growth everywhere.

1: A pink squat lobster (*Lauriea* sp.) blending in with its surroundings

2: An anemone shrimp (*Periclimenes holthuisi*)

3: This type of nudibranch (*Phyllidia varicosa*) can grow up to 7 centimetres.

4: The intricate structure of a sea fan (*Solenocaulon* sp.)

Sunnu's Lair

Location: Off the eastern side of the island

Average depth: 16 m

Maximum depth: 25 m

Dive rating:

Photo rating: 3, Macro

Unique features: Good coverage of hard and soft corals, sponges, nudibranchs

Hazards: None

This dive site derives its name from the local word for rock cod, which is found seasonally here in large numbers. Descending on the anchor buoy, the top of the reef is between 8 and 10 metres while the sandy bottom is 24 to 27 metres. Blue ribbontail stingrays beat a hasty retreat when approached too close. Small shoals of snappers and fusiliers mingle around red whip corals and small gorgonian fans. The richly covered top of the reef abounds with staghorn and lettuce corals, highlighted by sizeable tube corals and sponges. You will literally fall over the nudibranchs that come in a wide variety of colours and sizes, the largest of which is almost 18 centimetres.

Coral Garden

Location: Off the eastern side of the island

Average depth: 16 m

Maximum depth: 25 m

Dive rating: 🏊 🏊 🏊

Photo rating: 3, Wide angle; 4, Macro

Unique features: Hard and soft corals galore with plenty of reef inhabitants including the rare jawfish

Hazards: None

This site consists of a series of three patch reef structures. The tops of the structures are festooned with sponges, whip corals, staghorn corals and encrusting corals. The many crevices and gaps within the boulders are home to stonefish, scorpionfish and crocodile fish while blue-spotted rays camouflage themselves on the sandy bottom. A closer inspection of the site will reveal numerous nudibranchs, the very shy yellow boxfish, juvenile porcupinefish, pufferfish, cleaner shrimps and cleaner wrasses. The sandy gaps between the patch reefs are home to countless gobies, sea cucumbers and a rather shy jawfish that quickly retreats into its deep tunnel.

With barely a current to speak of, you can leisurely explore the good covering of acroporus, medium-sized boulders, encrusting corals, gorgonians, sea fans, sponges and ever-present featherstars. Other reef life includes football-sized frogfish, lobsters, schools of yellowtail snappers, catfish and orang-utan crabs.

1: The stalks and fleshy tissue of soft coral such as this (*Nepthea* sp.) can expand and contract.

2: A gigantic sea anemone (*Stichodactyla gigantea*)

Twin Rocks

Location: Off the southeastern side of the island

Average depth: 14 m

Maximum depth: 21 m

Dive rating:

Photo rating: 4, Macro

Unique features: Shoals of snappers and sweetlips, abundant corals

Hazards: None

1: A male ribbon eel (*Rhinomuraena quaesita*) trying to grab a small fish

2: Christmas tree worms (*Spirobranchus giganteus*)

3: A white-lined combtooth blenny (*Escenius bathi*)

Descending the buoy line to 21 metres, you will come to two patch reef formations. The smaller rock teems with shoals of small reef fish and the occasional jack. Perched on rocky outcrops, anemones host clownfish. White-lined lionfish lie in ambush between encrusting coral-covered boulders while bamboo sharks and coral sharks rest under crevices and cave-like openings. Traverse the sandy bottom to the larger rock, where patches of large gorgonians in hues of yellow and beige, whip corals and light blue tubular sponges with ever-present featherstars and boulders covered with Christmas trees feed in the current. Electric blue and black ribbon eels peek out of their sandy holes or sway in the gentle current. Pufferfish, groupers and fusiliers patrol the perimeter of the reef.

Twin City

Location: Off the eastern side of the island

Average depth: 17 m

Maximum depth: 24 m

Dive rating: 🤿 🤿 🤿

Photo rating: 4, Macro

Unique features: Jawfish, decorator crabs, shrimps, corals, sponges

Hazards: None

The sandy seabed of these two reef structures is home to a dozen blue ribbontail stingrays, blennies and shy jawfish. If the time is right, the jawfish may display its horde of eggs that it is carefully nesting in its mouth.

At around 18 metres, the upper stratum of the reef reveals a magnificent variety of hard and soft corals, colourful sponges, gorgonians and fans. Sea whips extend into the current and offer refuge to tiny coral shrimps. Decorator crabs that are easily missed, hingebeak shrimps and a variety of cleaner and coral shrimps are plentiful.

Mel's Place

Location: Off the eastern side of the island

Average depth: 13 m

Maximum depth: 19 m

Dive rating:

Photo rating: 4, Macro

Unique features: Jawfish, ribbon eels, squat lobsters, abundant shrimp population among corals and sponges

Hazards: None

There are large patches of staghorn, tube and brain corals throughout these two patch reefs. The gaps between the rocky outcrops are home to electric blue and black garden eels. Some coaxing will get the pink squat lobsters to ascend from the depths of the tubular sponges, although it might sometimes be difficult to distinguish them from the colour of their host. Whip corals sway in the light current with shoals of yellowtail snappers and fusiliers darting among them. In the upper region, anemones and their symbiotic clownfish, bubble corals with tiny translucent coral shrimps and nudibranchs can be seen.

1: The odd-looking jawfish (*Opistognathus* sp.) lives in a burrow and incubates eggs in its large mouth.

2: A gorgonian fan (*Subergorgia mollis*) projecting from the surface of the reef to catch the nutrient-rich current

3: Sharp eyes and patience will reward you with a glimpse of a pink squat lobster (*Lauriea* sp.), usually found inside barrel sponges.

Reef 77

Location: Southern side of the island

Average depth: 13 m

Maximum depth: 23 m

Dive rating:

Photo rating: 4, Wide angle

Unique features: Varied and dense population of soft corals, sponges, shoals of reef fish, leaffish, nudibranchs

Hazards: None

The slopes of this large patch reef have a healthy growth of sea fans and fragile gorgonians in hues of red and yellow. Paper-thin leaffish, almost unnoticed among the kaleidoscope of colours and shapes, sway in the slight current. The upper portion of the reef, at around 8 to 11 metres, is a feast for your eyes…and camera. Sponges, soft corals, encrusting and large table corals create a garden-like atmosphere for large shoals of snappers, fusiliers, groupers and catfish as well as dozens of butterflyfish, emperorfish and anglefish.

Other notable dive sites

Other sought-after sites include **Fan Rock**, **Catching Star** and **Veron Fan Garden**.

Three wrecks, namely **Mosquito Wreck** (believed to be a remnant of a Pacific warship) and **Lankayan Wreck** and **Jetty Wreck** (sunk to become artificial reefs), can be found in the waters around Pulau Lankayan and are frequented by groupers, jacks and black-tip sharks.

Left: A close-up of a tube anemone (*Cerianthidae* sp.), which achieves maximum growth in shallow, sun-lit waters

PULAU MATAKING

Coordinates: 04.35.10N, 118.57.34E

Left: A frogfish (*Antennarius pictus*) perched on sponges waits patiently for unsuspecting prey.

Inset: Sponges (*Axinellida auletta* sp.) are simple but efficient filter feeders.

Tucked away in the southeastern corner of Sabah, almost within visible range of the Philippine region of Mindanao, Pulau Mataking has started to gain a reputation for being an excellent place to dive in a completely relaxed and eco-friendly resort setting. The 20-hectare island is located in the Celebes Sea, about 30 kilometres east of the coastal town of Semporna, and is connected to the smaller island of Mataking Kecil by a sandbank that can be easily crossed during low tide. Alice Channel, a 100- to 150-metre crevice in the continental shelf connecting Pulau Mataking to the vast ocean depths of Pulau Sipadan, ensures a rich biodiversity of marine life.

Diving Pulau Mataking

The topography of the reefs of Pulau Mataking and the surrounding islands of Pandanan and Bohayan are essentially 45° slopes, descending to depths of 90 to 150 metres. The reef structures are made up predominantly of hard and soft corals, sea fans, gorgonians and small- to medium-sized boulders.

The practice of fish bombing has left its mark on some of the reefs, mostly in the western-facing areas. Fortunately, the area around Pulau Mataking has been declared a marine protected area so some of the affected reefs might recover, given time and adequate rehabilitation measures. The areas that have escaped destructive fishing practices, however, are pristine with a tremendous diversity of marine life.

Visibility and the quality of water are excellent. During spring tides, the dives invariably turn into drift dives with some sites sporting a significant down current that can catch the unprepared diver off-guard. Since diving the Mataking region is new, the marine life here, ranging from turtles to moray eels and clownfish, is rather shy, and a slow and patient approach is necessary, especially for photographers.

Below: Soft corals (*Siphonogorgia* sp.) find many nutrients in tidal currents sweeping the reef.

Facing page: Although primarily nocturnal, featherstars (*Comanthina audax*) will not miss an opportunity to feed if the currents are strong.

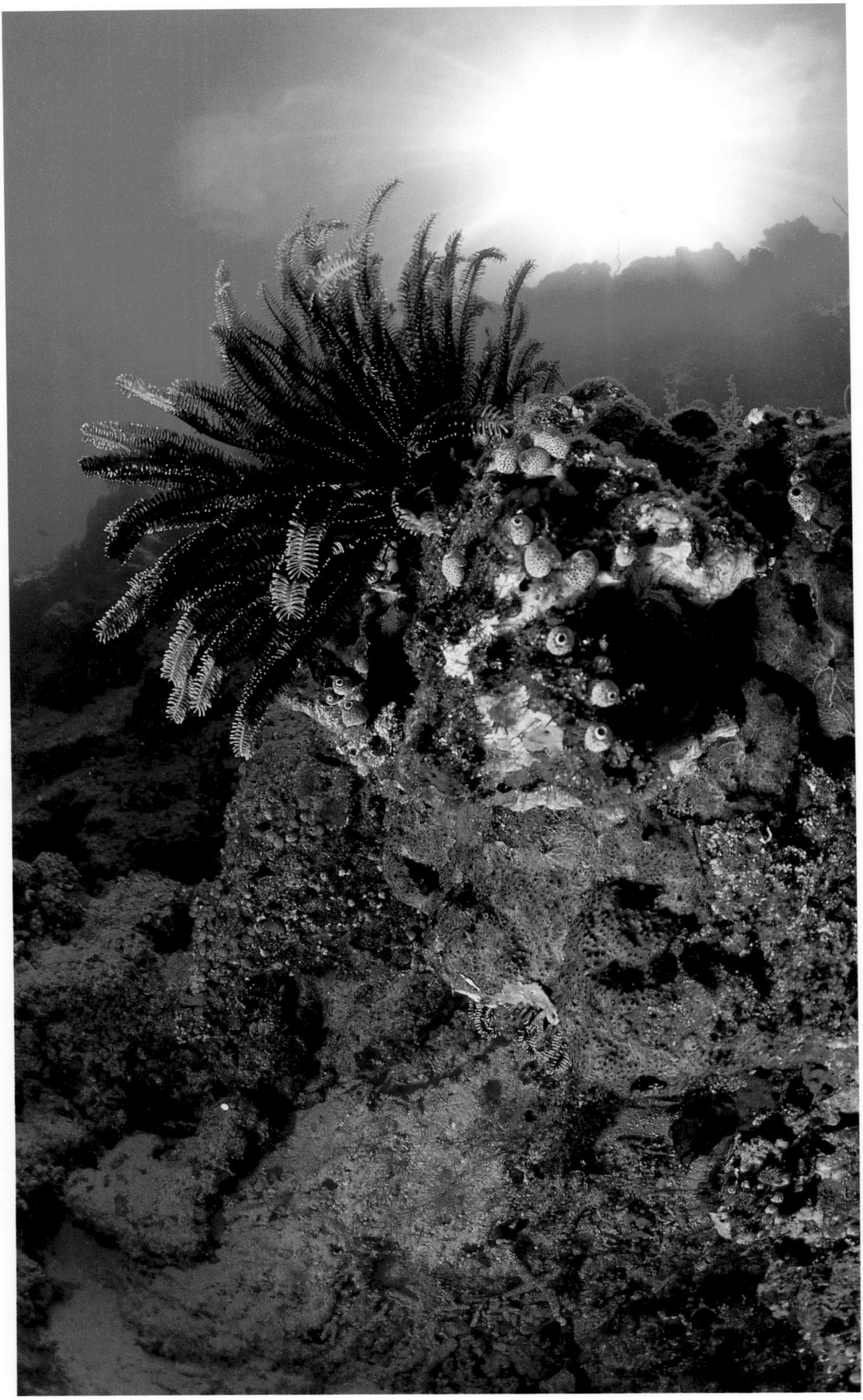

Getting There

Both Malaysia Airlines (www.malaysiaairlines.com) and AirAsia (www.airasia.com) operate daily direct flights from Kuala Lumpur to Tawau Airport. Alternatively, you can fly to Kota Kinabalu International Airport and then get a connecting flight to Tawau. The transfer from Tawau Airport to the coastal town of Semporna takes about 1 hour, followed by a 45-minute speedboat ride to Pulau Mataking.

Note: Security personnel from the Malaysian Armed Forces and police are very much in evidence, be it on land or sea. See also Security and Conservation on pages 194–195.

Accommodation

The Reef Dive Resort
Main Office: Ground Floor Wisma D.S.
No. 193–195 Jalan Bakau
91000 Tawau, Sabah
Tel: (60) 89 770 022 / (60) 89 770 023
Fax: (60) 89 763 270
Email: sales@mataking.com
Website: www.makating.com

Diving in Malaysia

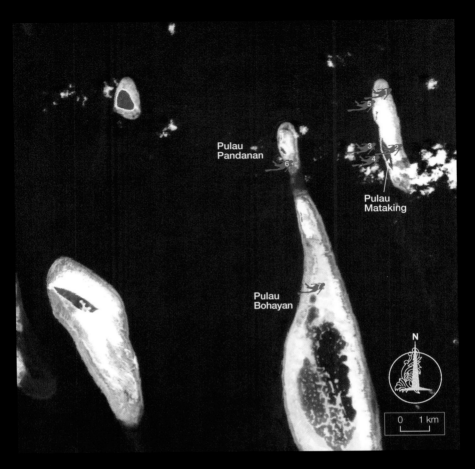

Pulau
Pandanan

Pulau
Mataking

Pulau
Bohayan

N

0   1 km

Key for Dive Sites

1: Turtle Playground
2: Coral Garden
3: Sweet Lips Rock

4: House Reef
5: Hump Head Point
6: Pandanan

7: Bohayan

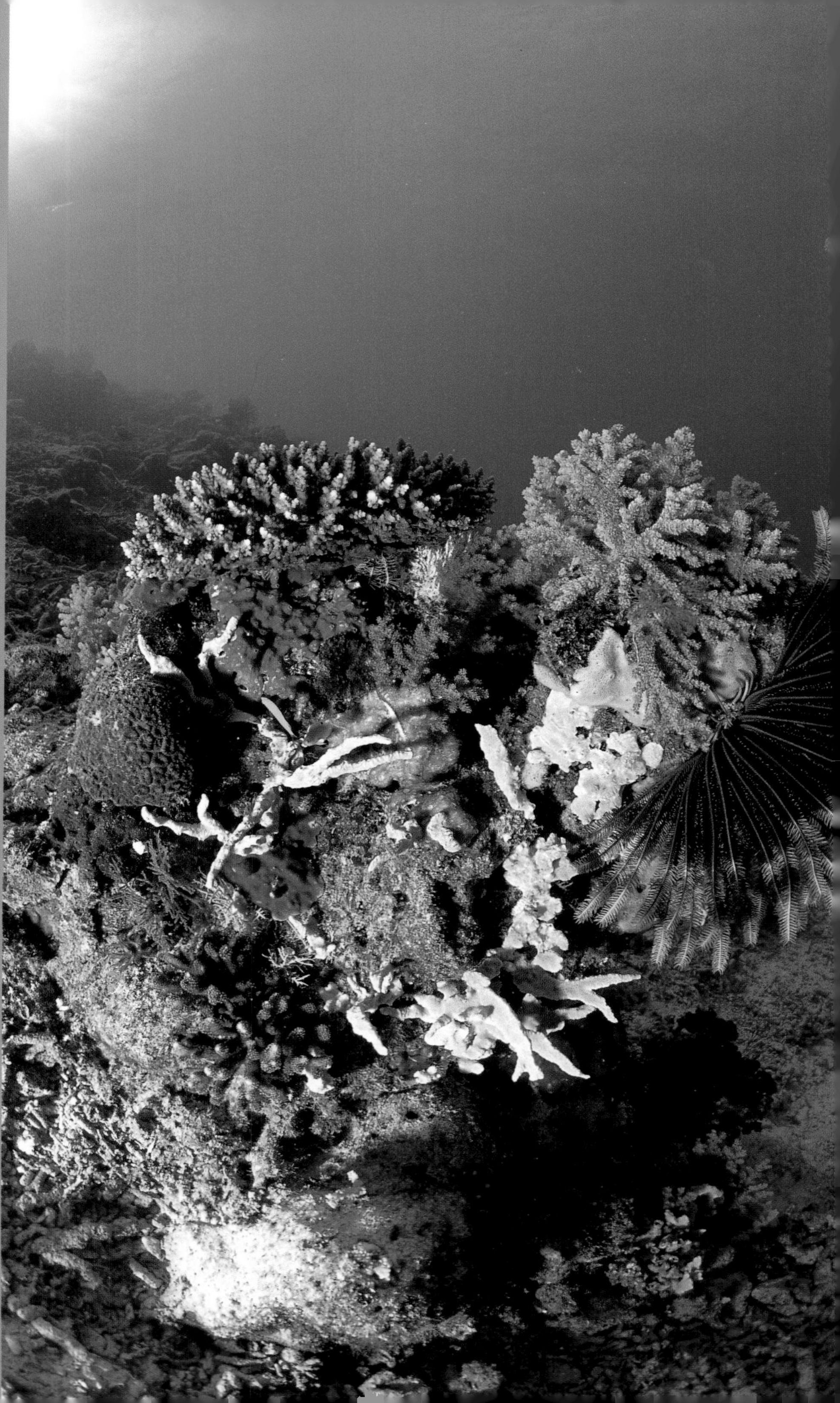

Turtle Playground

Location: 04.35.31N, 118.57.42E

Average depth: 25 m

Maximum depth: 35 m

Dive rating: 🤿 🤿 🤿

Photo rating: 3, Wide angle

Unique features: Gorgonians, featherstars, turtles, barracudas

Hazards: Tidal current can turn this into a drift dive

A mere 5-minute boat ride to the north of the jetty, this site is essentially a drift dive. Initially descending to 30 to 35 metres, the slopes present a healthy population of gorgonian fans extending into the current to feed. Green turtles and schools of yellowtail barracudas are frequently encountered. Making a gradual ascent, the upper reef is characterised by soft and encrusting corals, acroporus and an abundance of featherstars in a kaleidoscope of colours. Upon closer inspection of the boulders and coral formations, you will discover a multitude of inhabitants: lizardfish lying in wait for unsuspecting prey, colourful nudibranchs, magnificent tube worms and a large variety of reef fish.

Facing page: *Acropora*, soft coral varieties and featherstars (*Comanthina audax*) jockey for position.

Below: Sponges (*Callyspongia* sp.) often host a variety of other organisms.

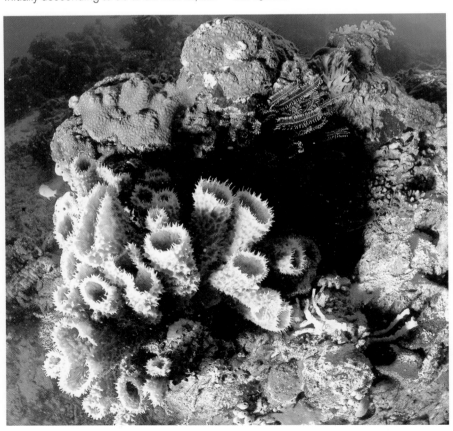

Coral Garden

Location: 04.35.00N, 118.57.42E

Average depth: 12 m

Maximum depth: 17 m

Dive rating: 🤿 🤿 🤿

Photo rating: 3, Wide angle

Unique features: Rich population of fans and soft corals, frogfish, lobsters

Hazards: None

The most spectacular site of Pulau Mataking is the eastern fringe of the island. The top of the reef, which lies just below the surface of the sea, drops gently to approximately 5 metres before it descends into the deeper region of the Alice Channel. Best dived during slack tide, the site is carpeted by soft corals that come in all colours and shapes as well as boasts a good covering of acroporus, medium-sized boulders, gorgonians, sea fans and sponges. Ever-present featherstars in a variety of colours, football-sized frogfish perched on sponges, glimpses of lobsters disappearing into crevices, schools of yellowtail snappers, catfish, orang-utan crabs hiding among bubble corals and a multitude of nudibranchs make for never-ending discoveries in a reef in full bloom.

1: Picturesque Alcyoniidae soft coral (*Sarcophyton* sp.)

2: Soft coral (*Scleronephthya* sp.)

Facing page: A congregation of *Acropora* species

Sweet Lips Rock

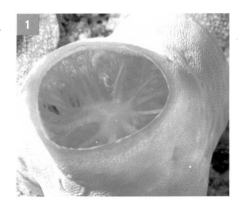

Location: 04.35.37N, 118.57.27E

Average depth: 15 m

Maximum depth: 17 m

Dive rating:

Photo rating: 3, Macro

Unique features: Small fans, juvenile reef fish, crustaceans, stonefish, mandarin fish

Hazards: None

Sweet Lips Rock is a 3-minute boat ride from the jetty and connects Pulau Mataking to Mataking Kecil. At a depth of around 8 metres, small, colourful and variously shaped sea fans and a variety of juvenile reef fish and crustaceans populate the reef slope. Even stonefish, crocodile fish, moray eels, cleaner shrimps, vertically poised razorfish and some hermit crabs have made their home among the corals and are very willing photographic subjects.

The prospect of watching the visually spectacular mandarin fish—an unusual, almost psychedelic coloured, species that only appears just before sunset—makes this site the logical choice for a night dive.

While diving the site, I was fortunate to observe ascidians releasing a cloud of tailed larvae. At first sight, it seemed as though smoke was rising from the tubular-shaped filter feeder. On closer inspection, I realised it was countless larvae forming a milky veil that drifted into the expanse of the reef.

1: A close-up of an ascidian (*Polycarpa aurata*)

2: Featherstars (*Stephanometra* sp.) are abundant in areas that have a strong current.

3: A nudibranch (*Chromodoris elizabethina*)

4: Ascidians (*Didemnum molle*) releasing tailed larvae which metamorphose within an hour

3

4

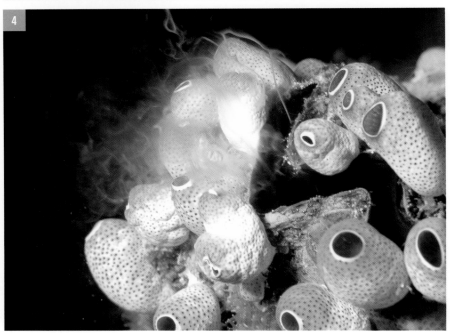

House Reef

Location: 04.35.10N, 118.57.29E

Average depth: 10 m

Maximum depth: 15 m

Dive rating: 🤿 🤿

Photo rating: 3, Macro

Unique features: Good variety of macro life

Hazards: None

For those divers who have an affinity for exploring macro life, the House Reef, just in front of the dive centre, will make for an interesting and relaxed dive. A teeming nursery for reef fish can be found between 5 and 12 metres among large rock boulders, cement blocks, metal frames and wooden logs (left over from the resort's construction). Marine life here includes juvenile groupers, emperorfish, pipefish, nudibranchs, gobies, wrasses and shrimps. In addition, a whale shark has been spotted passing about 20 metres from the reef house jetty. This is the perfect dive to finish off your diving trip to Pulau Mataking.

Other notable dive sites

There are about 14 dive sites around Pulau Mataking and the nearby islands of Pandanan and Bohayan. Among the most notable are **Hump Head Point** (04.35.39N, 118.57.26E), where you may encounter juvenile white-tip sharks, big-eye trevallies and the occasional green turtle; **Pandanan** (04.35.17N, 118.55.16E); and **Bohayan** (04.28.56N, 118.56.56E), where green turtles, soft corals, featherstars, snappers, batfish, countless schools of small reef fish, gorgonian fans and clown triggerfish move along the edge of the wall. Depending on the time of day, the upper reef is magnificent with its hard and soft corals.

1: Brittle stars (*Ophiothrix purpurea*) use their arms to filter planktonic animals and other food sources from the current.

2: Soft corals (*Dendronephthya* sp. and *Sinularia* sp.) and flower coral (*Xenia* sp.)

3: An anemone shrimp (*Thor amboinensis*)

4: This nudibranch (*Phyllidia ocellata*), from the Phyllidiidae suborder, lacks noticeable gills and has lumpy ridges on its back.

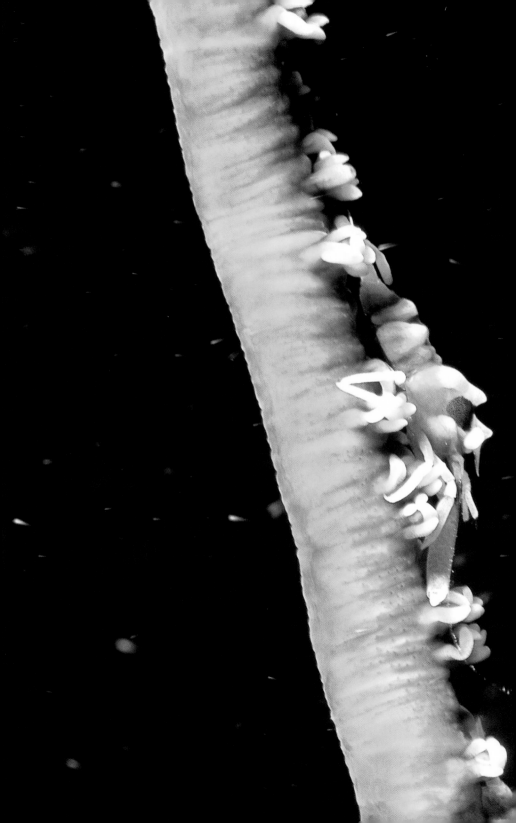

PULAU MABUL &
PULAU KAPALAI

Coordinates: 04.14.54N, 118.38.10E

Left: A symbiotic coral shrimp (*Dasycaris zanzibarica*) blending in with its coral host

Inset: A mitre shell (*Cantharus undosus*), commonly found in shallow water and under sand and rocks

Pulau Mabul, home to a rather derelict looking fishing village, and Pulau Kapalai, a mere sandbank that emerges during low tide, have become much sought-after destinations for macro life enthusiasts and are a dream for underwater macro photographers. They are extraordinary locations that boast an amazing variety of species, many of which are not found elsewhere in Malaysia. Species include pygmy sea horses, mandarin fish, flamboyant cuttlefish and mimic octopuses.

With its shallow reef profile, sandy seabed and patches of sea grass, Pulau Mabul, at first glance, does not look very inviting. Destructive fishing practices, notably dynamite and cyanide fishing, have had a devastating effect on the fringing reef surrounding the island; entire colonies of coral have been laid to waste. The local Bajau fishing community continues to use some of these practices, resulting in sharks and turtles being killed regularly. The marine life is also threatened by ongoing eco-unfriendly resort development.

Yet Pulau Mabul and, to a large extent, Pulau Kapalai (a 10-minute boat ride from Sipadan Water Village Jetty) have some very interesting sites populated by an incredible variety of nudibranchs, ribbon eels, ghost pipefish and shrimps of every description.

Even non-divers are not forgotten, although it is hard to resist the awe-inspiring beauty of the marine environment. Snorkelling and other water sports, beach volleyball, visiting the small Bajau fishing village in the central part of the island or just lazing around will keep every guest occupied.

With the increasing number of divers visiting the islands, the stress on the reef environment has become even more evident. Reef management initiatives such as coral planting projects to rehabilitate reefs, self policing and clean-up campaigns are a few of the measures that have been set up to help to maintain the region's reputation as one of the best dive destinations in the world.

With the impending closure of resorts on Pulau Sipadan, Pulau Mabul has become the alternative location for some of Pulau Sipadan's dive operators. As space is a premium, one can expect that the sleepy fishing village and its community will come under increasing pressure from resort developers to relocate.

Diving Pulau Mabul and Pulau Kapalai

At first glance, the dive sites around Pulau Mabul are rather mediocre as they are

shallow with a sandy bottom and have very few walls or slopes that descend to around 30 metres. The mostly shallow bottom also accounts for frequent poor visibility, especially at the house reefs where dozens of divers congregate to look for the more unusual inhabitants of Pulau Mabul's seabed. It is advisable to dive in buddy pairs and, if you beg long enough, under the guidance of the local dive masters who are extremely accomplished naturalists. Night dives are a must as the reef comes alive with an incredible variety of nocturnal creatures. Again, diving in buddy pairs or very small groups is best if you are taking underwater shots so you can avoid getting a diver's fin in the corner of your prized shot.

To call Pulau Kapalai an island is probably a misnomer. It is not really an island

Above: Pulau Mabul and Pulau Kapalai captivate with their seemingly endless varieties of nudibranch such as *Chromodoris*.

Facing page: A colourful nudibranch (*Bonellidae*) clinging to a coral stem

but rather the upper stratum of an underlying reef structure topped by a sandbank that only emerges during low tide. The Kapalai reef system, although damaged in certain areas by past destructive fishing, features a host of easy-to-explore dive sites that make for never-ending discoveries of unique marine life.

Getting There

Both Malaysia Airlines (www.malaysiaairlines.com) and AirAsia (www.airasia.com) operate daily direct flights from Kuala Lumpur to Tawau Airport. Alternatively, you can fly to Kota Kinabalu International Airport and then get a connecting flight to Tawau. The transfer from Tawau Airport to the coastal town of Semporna takes about 1 hour, followed by a 40-minute speedboat ride to Pulau Mabul or a 45-minute ride to Pulau Kapalai.

Note: Security personnel from the Malaysian Armed Forces and police are very much in evidence, be it on land or sea. See also Security and Conservation on pages 194–195.

Accommodation

ON PULAU MABUL
Sipadan Water Village Resort
P.O. Box No. 62156
91031 Tawau, Sabah
Tel: (60) 89 752 996
Fax: (60) 89 752997
Email: swv@sipadan-village.com.my
Website: www.sipadan-village.com.my

Sipadan Mabul Resort
2nd Floor, Lot 8, Block B
Jalan Padas, Segama Complex
88000 Kota Kinabalu, Sabah
Tel: (60) 88 230 006
Fax: (60) 88 242 003
Email: mabul@po.jaring.my
Website: www.sipadan-mabul.com.my

Borneo Divers Mabul Resort
Locked Bag 194
88999 Kota Kinabalu, Sabah
Tel: (60) 88 222 226/ (60) 88 222 227
Fax: (60) 88 221 550
Email: information@borneodivers.info
Website: www.borneodivers.info

ON PULAU KAPALAI
Sipadan-Kapalai Dive Resort (Kapalai Water Village)
Pulau Sipadan Resort & Tours Sdn Bhd.
484 Bandar Sabindo, PO Box No 61120
91021 Tawau, Sabah
Tel: (60) 89 765 200
Fax: (60) 89 763 575/ (60) 89 763 563
Email: info@sepilok.com

Key for Dive Sites

1: Paradise

2: Ribbon Valley

3: Seaventures Platform

4: Eel Garden

5: Lobster Wall

6: Mandarin Valley

Paradise

Location: 04.14.54N, 118.38.10E (Sipadan Water Village Jetty)

Average depth: 8 m

Maximum depth: 18 m

Dive rating: 🤿 🤿 🤿 🤿

Photo rating: 5, Macro

Unique features: One of a kind! Strange and rare macro life galore

Take note: Addictive and heavy on film

Hazards: None

This is the house reef of Sipadan Water Village Resort and is definitely one of the most frequently dived sites in Pulau Mabul. At first glance, the sandy bottom with its occasional submerged palm tree, old tyres, oil drums and cement blocks does not seem to be a worthwhile location to explore. However, the algae patches on the seafloor below the second buoy to the right as seen from the jetty house a variety of macro life forms. These range from sea horses that blend in with the fleshy leaves of the green algae, ghost pipefish, frogfish, sea moths, spotted-face moray eels hiding under the cement block, juvenile cuttlefish, black-saddled tobies, yellow-spotted burrfish to snake and ribbon eels.

Tracking left and staying at a depth of about 10 to 12 metres, a rock formation with medium-sized boulders with encrusting corals, sponges and acroporus (many of which have been planted by visitors to the resort in recent years) are home to flamboyant cuttlefish, ghost shrimps, orang-utan crabs, anemone clownfish, decorator crabs and a number of reef fish species. Where the boulders meet the sandy bottom, triggerfish, lionfish, trumpetfish, pufferfish and porcupinefish patrol the perimeter.

If possible, ask your dive master to take you on a dive below the second jetty to catch the spectacle of the perpetually mating, multi-coloured mandarin fish which make a brief cameo appearance just before sunset. Night dives at Paradise are spectacular but you should go in buddy pairs as visibility becomes very poor due to the stirred-up sand caused by ever eager photographers who jostle for positions for that 'shot of a lifetime'.

During spring tides and periods of heavy rain over inland areas, the waters around Sipadan Water Village Resort can become contaminated with flotsam that comes from the river flowing into the Semporna estuary and the numerous water villages fringing the coastline.

Facing page: A delightful thorny sea horse (*Hippocampus histrix*)

Below: An electric blue ribbon eel (*Rhinomuranena quaesita*), which is rarely seen leaving its burrow

Ribbon Valley

Location: Southern tip of Mabul Reef

Average depth: 12 m

Maximum depth: 18 m

Dive rating:

Photo rating: 3, Wide angle; 4, Macro

Unique features: Gorgonians, rays, rich diversity of reef fish, stonefish, crocodile fish, scorpionfish

Hazards: None

The southern tip of Pulau Mabul experiences somewhat stronger currents than elsewhere around the island. Consequently, this means there is better visibility. The terraced reef slopes to the sandy bottom at about 25 to 30 metres, making this one of the deeper dives of Pulau Mabul.

Gorgonians, sea fans and soft corals that feed in the nutrient-rich current account for the greater diversity and density of reef fish. Large numbers of butterflyfish, damselfish, emperorfish, angelfish and parrotfish make for never-ending photo opportunities. The sandy areas topping the terraces reveal a large number of the reef's camouflage experts: stonefish, crocodile fish and scorpionfish blend almost indistinguishably among the surrounding rocks and corals while gobies, blennies and moray eels hide in every conceivable crack and crevice. Blue-spotted ribbontail stingrays and giant reef rays burrow into the sand and are always on the lookout for prey.

Seaventures Platform

Location: About 300 m north of Sipadan Water Village Jetty

Average depth: 17 m

Maximum depth: 18 m

Dive rating: 🤿 🤿 🤿 🤿

Photo rating: 4, Macro

Unique features: Moray eels, crocodile fish, mantis shrimps, stonefish, frogfish, leaffish

Hazards: Strong tidal current

This interesting and unusual dive site is just below the platform of Seaventures Dive Resort (a 5-minute boat ride from Mabul Water Village). The maximum depth of this site is 18 to 22 metres but is best dived during slack tide as the currents can be rather challenging to the less experienced diver. An amazing variety of marine life has made its home among cement blocks, rusty steel pipes and metal sheets below the platform. Football-sized frogfish, paper-thin leaffish, stonefish, crocodile fish, moray eels (you must meet the resident giant moray eel that has been named Elvis by the dive masters), parrotfish, butterflyfish, barracudas and mantis shrimps are just some of the species populating this area. A word of caution: Exercise good buoyancy control and stay off the bottom and away from the various structures as it is easy to mistake a stonefish or crocodile fish for just another rock or piece of discarded construction equipment.

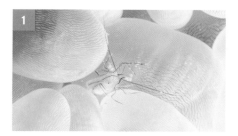

Eel Garden

Location: Southwestern fringe of Mabul Reef

Average depth: 15 m

Maximum depth: 20 m

Dive rating: 🐟 🐟 🐟

Photo rating: 4, Macro

Unique features: Garden eel colonies, ribbon eels, frogfish, mantis shrimps

Hazards: None

Located towards the southern end of Pulau Mabul, Eel Garden is one of the more traditional deeper dives. A sandy plateau at around 22 metres, which continues to drop away towards the open sea, features a few meagre coral formations that break the monotony of the seascape. As with most other dive sites around Pulau Mabul, try to avoid kicking up the silty bottom so that you can observe gobies seeking refuge in the tiny crevices and moray eels occupying larger holes. What appears to be blades of sea grass swaying with the current near the sandy patch turn out to be colonies of elusive garden eels which quickly dart back into their burrows as soon as they detect approaching shadows or excessive movement in the water. Brightly coloured gobies, cohabiting with the obsessive cleaning Alpheus shrimp, rare lemon-coloured moray eels, well-camouflaged frogfish and electric blue ribbon eels occupy the upper stratum of the reef. Large holes in the sandy floor hide the gigantic mantis shrimp, a fierce predatory crustacean that you should approach with caution.

1: A coral shrimp (*Vir philippinensis*) among bubble corals—a rewarding sight for the patient observer

2: Well-camouflaged crocodile fish (*Cymbacephalus beauforti*) lying in wait for unsuspecting prey

3: 'Elvis', the very approachable resident giant moray (*Gymnothorax javanicus*)

Lobster Wall

Location: Southwestern edge of Mabul Reef

Average depth: 18 m

Maximum depth: 22 m

Dive rating: 🐸 🐸 🐸

Photo rating: 4, Macro

Unique features: Lobsters, nudibranchs, frogfish, gorgonians, sea fans

Hazards: None

Lobster Wall rounds the outer boundaries of the southwestern edge of Mabul Reef. It is the closest Pulau Mabul has to a vertical wall dive location. The site reaches a depth of 40 metres and, depending on the direction of the prevailing current, can become a drift dive. Descending to around 21 metres, the wall features numerous grottos, cavities, balconies and small recesses. Gorgonians and varieties of soft and encrusting corals are home to small but always fascinating species. Among the intricate and fragile branches of *Acropora* are shoals of squirrelfish, butterflyfish, soldierfish and coral groupers. Shy boxfish, pufferfish and black-saddled tobies dart in and out of their hiding places while the long antennae of shy lobsters protrude from the many holes and caves dotting the wall. Perfectly camouflaged frogfish perched on coral outcrops are easily overlooked among the numerous nudibranchs, flatworms, tiny bubble shrimps and other crustaceans. Although Lobster Wall does not have the abundant pelagic species that characterise wall dives at Pulau Sipadan, it is nevertheless a site that shines through with its splendour and diversity.

Mandarin Valley

Location: Northeastern tip of Kapalai Reef

Average depth: 12 m

Maximum depth: 18 m

Dive rating: 🤿 🤿 🤿

Photo rating: 3, Macro

Unique features: Variety of corals, stonefish, frogfish, nudibranchs, mandarin fish, octopuses

Hazards: None

Entering the water at the end of Sipadan-Kapalai Dive Resort Jetty, keep the gently sloping reef to your left and descend to approximately 12 metres. Here, you will notice a diverse population of corals supporting many species of colourful coral-dwelling fish and invertebrates that are intermingled with numerous mollusc species including giant clams. Octopuses emerging at night to hunt for food hide in crevices when you approach but, if in luck, you might catch a glimpse of some quickly retreating tentacles. Sponges and crinoids dot the sandy patches which are home to frogfish, cuttlefish, ghost pipefish and parrotfish.

If you cross the sandy valley-like gap in the seabed, you will come to an area punctuated by rocky structures and ablaze with gorgonians, anemones, soft corals and sponges. Camouflaged by the rocks and hidden in the crevices are favourites of a photographer—nudibranchs, shrimps, leaffish, lionfish, stonefish, frogfish, gobies, ghost pipefish, delightful nudibranchs and the shy mandarin fish.

1: A spider crab (*Acheus japonicus*), also called an orang-utan crab by locals, among grape-like bubble corals

2: The bright colours of this polyclad flatworm (*Pseudoceros bifurcus*) warn predators that it is poisonous.

3: A solitary ascidian (*Polycarpa aurata*)

PULAU SIPADAN

Coordinates: 04.07.02N, 118.37.51E

Left: Descending to a depth of over 600 metres, the famed walls of Pulau Sipadan are home to rich marine life.

Inset: Mighty gorgonian fans (*Subergorgia mollis*) sometimes reach a span of almost 3 metres.

Pulau Sipadan, located 35 kilometres southeast of the coastal town of Semporna and made famous by Jacques Cousteau's *Ghost of the Sea Turtles* (1989) and Michael Patrick Wong's book *Sipadan— Borneo's Underwater Paradise* (1991), is an oceanic island that drops to a depth of about 700 metres. It is only 14 hectares in size.

Geologically, the island structure dates back to the Palaeocene period when there were massive tectonic movements and volcanic activity. The narrow underwater fringing reef that encircles Pulau Sipadan to a depth of around 30 metres suggests that the island was significantly higher about 20,000 years ago compared to today's elevation of 2 metres above sea level. The constant upwelling of nutrients from the sea sustains an incredible diversity and density of marine life, including, among others, schools of pelagic species. Over 500 species of coral and about 3000 species of fish have been identified so far.

Over the past 10 years, Pulau Sipadan has become one of the most sought-after dive destinations worldwide, attracting visitors, photographers and researchers from all over the world.

Diving Pulau Sipadan

Diving in Pulau Sipadan is dynamic and constantly changing. Although you should not expect blue waters and visibility of 50 metres on every dive, what you will find below the surface will take your breath away. Pulau Sipadan is one of the few dive destinations in Asia where you are guaranteed encounters with an amazing array of marine life every time you choose to dive there. Each dive holds the promise of the encounter of a lifetime, be it in the form of nudibranchs, ribbon eels, gobies, about 500 coral species, jacks, barracudas, green turtles, hawksbill turtles or the abundant black-tip and white-tip reef sharks. In addition, it is not uncommon to come across schools of dolphins playing in the wake of the boat and, during certain months, migrating sperm and pilot whales as well as the occasional whale shark. For photographers, it would be a good idea to keep a few frames or memory reserved in your camera for such encounters.

It is probably necessary at this point to dispel the common misconception that diving Pulau Sipadan is only for the advanced or experienced diver. It is safe for all certified divers, including those with entry-level open water certification, to dive Pulau Sipadan within the limits of the training they have received. Dive operations are normally conducted from twin-engine mono-hull dive boats that accommodate up to 10 divers. Descents to the dive sites are done without the aid of a descent line so you should avoid lingering on the surface to ensure you do not drift away from the site into the open sea.

Security and Conservation

The highly publicised kidnapping of tourists from Pulau Sipadan in 2000 brought virtually all tourism to the island to a halt. In the wake of this and successive kidnappings, the Malaysian authorities have enforced extensive security measures in the area. Now, navy and marine police boats regularly patrol the area around

Above: Schooling big-eye trevallies (*Caranx sexfasciatus*), one of Pulau Sipadan's special treats

Pulau Sipadan and neighbouring islands such as Pulau Mabul and Pulau Kapalai. In some instances, the police have even set up permanent bases adjacent to resorts.

With tourism to Pulau Sipadan picking up again, the Malaysian government began to formulate plans to designate the island and its surrounding waters as a marine park in 2003. These plans aim to put a stop to the environmentally damaging resort developments of the past. As an immediate measure, the existing resorts have been given notice to vacate the island and are expected to do so by the end of 2004. These resorts will probably relocate to nearby Pulau Mabul which has resorts ranging from the basic to the luxurious.

Getting There

Both Malaysia Airlines (www.malaysiaairlines.com) and AirAsia (www.airasia.com) operate daily direct flights from Kuala Lumpur to Tawau Airport. Alternatively, you can fly to Kota Kinabalu International Airport and then get a connecting flight to Tawau. The transfer from Tawau Airport to the coastal town of Semporna takes about 1 hour, followed by a 40-minute speedboat ride to neighbouring Pulau Mabul.

Accommodation

ON PULAU MABUL

Sipadan Water Village Resort
P.O. Box No. 62156
91031 Tawau, Sabah
Tel: (60) 89 752 996
Fax: (60) 89 752997
Email: swv@sipadan-village.com.my
Website: www.sipadan-village.com.my

Sipadan Mabul Resort
2nd Floor, Lot 8, Block B
Jalan Padas, Segama Complex
88000 Kota Kinabalu, Sabah
Tel: (60) 88 230 006
Fax: (60) 88 242 003
Email: mabul@po.jaring.my
Website: www.sipadan-mabul.com.my

Borneo Divers Mabul Resort
Locked Bag 194
88999 Kota Kinabalu, Sabah
Tel: (60) 88 222 226/ (60) 88 222 227
Fax: (60) 88 221 550
Email: information@borneodivers.info
Website: www.borneodivers.info

ON PULAU KAPALAI

Sipadan-Kapalai Dive Resort (Kapalai Water Village)
Pulau Sipadan Resort & Tours Sdn Bhd.
484 Bandar Sabindo, PO Box No 61120
91021 Tawau, Sabah
Tel: (60) 89 765 200
Fax: (60) 89 763 575/ (60) 89 763 563
Email: info@sepilok.com

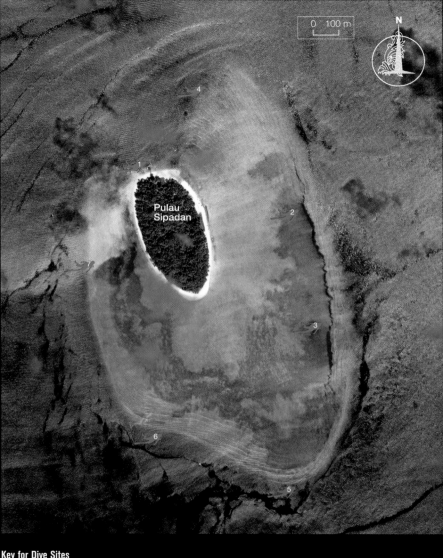

0   100 m

N

Pulau
Sipadan

Key for Dive Sites

1: The Drop-Off   4: Barracuda Point   7: Hanging Gardens
2: Coral Gardens   5: South Point

The Drop-Off

Location: 04.07.04N, 118.37.52E

Average depth: 15 m

Maximum depth: 21 m

Dive rating: 🐬 🐬 🐬 🐬 🐬

Photo rating: 4, Wide angle; 4, Macro at night

Unique features: Many large turtles, reef sharks, soft corals, macro life

Hazards: Can get busy; be aware of boats approaching the jetty; DO NOT ENTER THE TURTLE TOMB

One of the famed dive sites of Pulau Sipadan, the Drop-Off is what might be considered the house reef of the island. Only a few metres from the sandy beach, the wall drops to a dizzying depth of over 700 metres. Even just snorkelling off the beach while passing time between dives will reward you with a truly magnificent sight

as turtles and sharks pass just metres away amidst a backdrop of corals and colourful reef fish.

Rather than being a bare rock face, the wall features numerous grottos, cavities, balconies and small recesses that teem with corals and macro life. Large gorgonians and varieties of soft and encrusting corals are home to moray eels, lionfish, batfish, gobies, clownfish and crustaceans. Solitary barracudas, parrotfish, juvenile big-eye trevallies, white-tip reef sharks, green turtles and hawksbill turtles cruise just off the wall.

If you keep the wall to your right, you will come to the entrance of the famous Turtle Tomb at a depth of 21 metres. There is a very visible sign next to the entrance that warns too adventurous divers of the hazards of venturing into the cave without a guide. Over the years, some divers have met the same fate as the many turtles whose skeletons litter the floor of the cave.

It is important to remember not to stray too far off the wall or to drift too far

horizontally as currents, at times, can sweep you past Barracuda Point to the right or North Point to the left.

Night dives at the Drop-Off, which explore the shallow region between 5 and 10 metres, are highly recommended. The incessant clicking, ticking and crunching noises of crustaceans and other reef life accompany the magnificent display of nocturnal activity. Among the more common sights are shrimps, scorpionfish, bumphead parrotfish sleeping in cracks in the wall and razorfish hiding in the branches of gorgonians.

1: Stunted coral growth and rubble, both signs of excessive use

2: Hard coral heads (*Porites*) are home to many types of marine life.

3: Sponges (*Haliclona fascigera* and *Xestospongia testudinaria*), the reef's vacuum cleaners, extract bacteria and similar microscopic life forms from the passing currents.

Coral Gardens

Location: Northeastern side of the island

Average depth: 7 m

Maximum depth: 10 m

Dive rating: 🐋 🐋 🐋 🐋

Photo rating: 4, Wide angle; 4, Macro

Unique features: Soft corals, orang-utan crabs, nudibranchs, yellowtail snappers

Hazards: None

A spectacular site of Pulau Sipadan is the eastern side of the island. The reef initially drops gently to approximately 5 metres and then descends into the depths of the Sipadan abyss. With barely a current to speak of, a visual feast of soft corals in every colour and shape, a good covering of acroporus, medium-sized boulders, encrusting corals, gorgonians, sea fans and ever-present featherstars give the reef a festive look. Football-sized frogfish perched on an acroporus outcrop, lobsters disappearing into deep caves, schools of yellowtail snappers, catfish, orang-utan crabs hiding among bubble corals and a multitude of nudibranchs make for never-ending discoveries in a reef at its best.

1: Magnificent soft corals (*Dendronephthya*) decorate the underwater walls and reef slopes of Pulau Sipadan.

2: A multicoloured leaf scorpionfish (*Taenianotus triacanthus*) camouflaged next to an ascidian filter feeder

3: Pulau Sipadan's trademark green turtle (*Chelonia mydas*)

4: A white-tip reef shark (*Triaenodon obesus*) at one of numerous cleaning stations

White-Tip Avenue

Location: Eastern fringe of the island

Average depth: 25 m

Maximum depth: 40 m

Dive rating: 🤿 🤿 🤿 🤿 🤿

Photo rating: 4, Wide angle

Unique features: Gorgonians, black corals, grey reef sharks, hammerhead sharks

Hazards: None

Located off the eastern part of Pulau Sipadan, White-Tip Avenue has a terrace-like upper reef structure that teems with corals and reef fish. This is followed by a sudden drop into the deep sea. The typical dive profile for this site will see you descending to around 30 to 35 metres. As you make your descent, you will pass large gorgonians, polyps feeding in the current, black corals and a multitude of sponges, groupers, triggerfish, boxfish, butterflyfish and parrotfish. Directing your attention to the open sea, grey reef sharks cruise the wall and, if in luck, you will see a school of majestic scalloped hammerhead sharks that frequent the deeper regions of Pulau Sipadan's waters.

Barracuda Point

Location: Northern tip of the island

Average depth: 17 m

Maximum depth: 35 m

Dive rating: 🤿 🤿 🤿 🤿 🤿

Photo rating: 5, Wide angle

Unique features: Schools of barracudas and jacks, white-tip reef sharks

Hazards: Sometimes swift currents require experience

The famous Barracuda Point is one of Sipadan's premier dive sites. Usually, you enter the water at the eastern tip of the island and, keeping the wall to your right, drift with the current to level off at about 25 metres. The wall drops vertically to about 600 metres, with the exception of a ledge that extends from 17 to 25 metres. This ledge acts as a perfect observation point to the spectacle unfolding before you.

During early morning dives or periods when the thermocline rises, you can catch glimpses of grey reef and scalloped hammerhead sharks cruising off the wall at a depth of around 35 metres and below. During afternoon dives, a large school of barracudas, numbering about 1000 to 2000, usually make an appearance. Lazily moving against the current, the cone-shaped school will slowly close around you, enfolding you in a mass of sleek, silvery bodies. On occasions when the barracudas decide to entertain elsewhere, a large school of jacks and a dozen or more white-tip reef sharks may cruise by. Triggerfish, green turtles, batfish, bumphead parrotfish and fusiliers also abound.

Drifting up to the shallower region of the reef, macro life like nudibranchs, soft

and hard corals, sponges, parrotfish, angelfish, flute fish and the occasional leopard shark provide ample photo opportunities.

1: A school of big-eye trevallies (*Caranx sexfasciatus*) congregating along the drop-off

2: An expanse of *Acropora* hard coral surrounded by a myriad of cardinalfish (*Apogonidae*)

3: A breathtaking display of schooling chevron barracudas (*Sphyraena putnamiae*) in classical tornado formation

South Point

Location: Southern tip of the island

Average depth: 17 m

Maximum depth: 35 m

Dive rating: 🐟 🐟 🐟 🐟

Photo rating: 4, Wide angle

Unique features: Schools of barracudas and jacks, reef sharks

Hazards: Current can challenge the less experienced diver

South Point is another not-to-be-missed dive site. During recent trips, it has been the most likely site for seeing shoals of jacks and barracudas. It is usually a drift dive.

If you keep the wall to your right, it is not uncommon to run into large schools of jacks at depths of 6 to 12 metres. Continuing to the lower regions of around 28 to 32 metres, a school of barracudas, probably shuttling between this site and Barracuda Point, can be seen quite regularly. Drifting with the current, you can try to enter the school from the top and slowly drop into the centre while the school forms a 'cyclone' around you.

South Point has a few sandy areas at 20 to 30 metres that are preferred resting places and cleaning stations for leopard sharks and white-tip sharks but it does not feature any spectacular coral formations at its lower depths. However, ascending diagonally to a depth of 5 to 8 metres, a splendid coral garden provides the perfect backdrop for the safety stop. Turtles feeding on corals, batfish, sweetlips, juvenile white-tip sharks, leaf scorpionfish and other reef dwellers can be observed.

All: Hundreds of schooling big-eye trevallies (*Caranx sexfasciatus*) in close formation, a highlight of diving Pulau Sipadan

Staghorn Crest

Location: Southwestern tip of the island

Average depth: 25 m

Maximum depth: 35 m

Dive rating: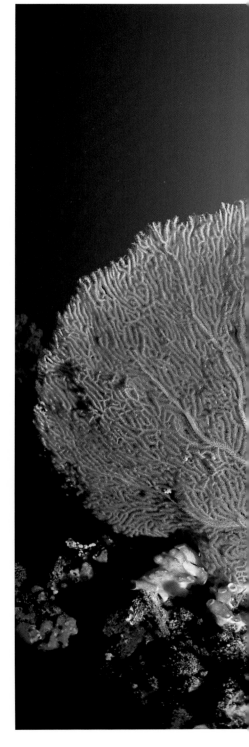

Photo rating: 4, Wide angle

Unique features: Sea fans, black corals, grey reef sharks, hammerhead sharks

Hazards: Watch no decompression limit (NDL) multilevel dive restrictions

An excellent wall dive in true Sipadan fashion, this site is best dived in the afternoon. The dive begins with a descent to the maximum depth of around 35 metres. (Remember to watch no decompression limit (NDL) multilevel dive restrictions.) The wall is broken by ledges, crevices and balconies populated by colourful sea fans, gorgonians, large barrel sponges and dense black corals. Heading away from the wall into the open sea, look into the deep end where you might spot grey reef sharks, scalloped hammerheads and, during the right season, manta rays. Following the classic dive profile, i.e. ascending to the upper region, shoals of jacks and barracudas are spectacular sights.

Diving in Malaysia

Right: A majestic gorgonian fan (*Subergorgia mollis*) in the nutrient-rich waters of Pulau Sipadan

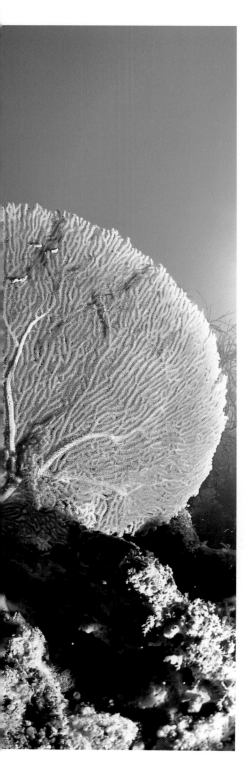

Hanging Gardens

Location: Northwestern side of the island

Average depth: 15 m

Maximum depth: 17 m

Dive rating: 🤿 🤿 🤿 🤿

Photo rating: 4, Wide angle

Unique features: Large, richly coloured soft corals, gorgonians, pelagic species

Hazards: Can become a drift dive

A steep wall dive with the drop-off just below the surface, Hanging Garden derives its name from the large groups of alcyonarian soft corals that feed on the rich nutrients in the current. The crevices and cracks of the wall are adorned with large gorgonians making for spectacular up-angle photographs into the sun. In the deeper region, reef sharks, leopard sharks and hammerheads make cameo appearances. Large green turtles are ever present, either taking a nap in the many recesses or serenely drifting in the current. Moray eels are often seen peering out of their lairs as are blue-spotted ribbontail stingrays camouflaged in the sandy patches. A closer inspection of the wall will reveal colourful nudibranchs, gobies and many more reef residents.

TUNKU ABDUL RAHMAN MARINE PARK

Coordinates: 05.57.5N, 115.59.4E

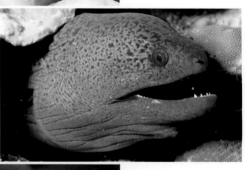

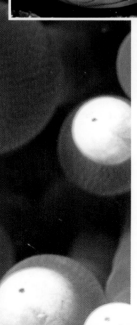

Left: An anemonefish (*Amphiprion* sp.) and a sea anemone living in symbiotic harmony

Inset: The giant moray (*Gymnothorax javanicus*) is one of the largest types of moray eel and can grow to a length of almost 3 metres.

Tunku Abdul Rahman Marine Park, located just 3 kilometres from the coastal city of Kota Kinabalu, consists of a group of five islands: Gaya, Manukan, Mamutik, Sapi and Sulug. The park was gazetted in 1974 and now covers an area of approximately 50 square kilometres. Terrestrial features of the park include mangroves, coastal forest and stretches of sandy beaches with rich flora and fauna including reptiles and sea eagles. Fringing reefs with gentle slopes surround the islands.

Apart from diving, there is plenty to see and do in Kota Kinabalu. The northeastern part of the city is often referred to as Old KK and is bordered by Jalan Gaya and Jalan Pantai. Jalan Gaya has an interesting street market every Sunday, and the two nearby shopping complexes of Sinsuron and Segama are also worth visiting. Signal Hill Observatory is located at Jalan Padang and casts its shadow over the Atkinson Clock Tower.

There is plenty on offer for outdoor enthusiasts in and around Kota Kinabalu. Thousands of people each year climb Mount Kinabalu, the highest peak in Southeast Asia at 4101 metres. Known in ancient times as Aki Nabalu (Home of the Spirit of the Departed), the mountain has UNESCO World Heritage status. The highest point, now called Low's Peak, was conquered by John Whitehead in 1888. A round-trip climb usually takes 2 days. The first night's accommodation at Laban Rata Resthouse on Panar Laban Plateau (3000 metres) can be reached in 3 to 6 hours. It is usual to get up at 2.30 am the next morning for the final leg towards the summit so that a spectacular view of the sunrise can be enjoyed. Climbers who proceed beyond Laban Rata need the compulsory service of a guide. Equally stunning is the sight of Low's Gully, a chasm in the mountain that drops 1500 metres.

Attractions for non-climbers include 20 kilometres of trails around the headquarters of Kinabalu National Park while ardent botanists can explore, among others, the labelled plants in Mountain Garden or specimens of the park's flora and fauna housed in the Exhibit Centre. Poring Hot Springs, which is 40 kilometres southeast of Kinabalu National Park headquarters, provides relief for tired muscles in its natural hot pools. Nearby attractions include a butterfly farm, Kipungit Falls and a canopy walk.

Diving Tunku Abdul Rahman Marine Park

Diving can be a year-round affair at Tunku Abdul Rahman Marine Park, although November through February experience wet and windy conditions due to the northeast monsoon. Visibility throughout the year ranges from 10 to 15 metres but it

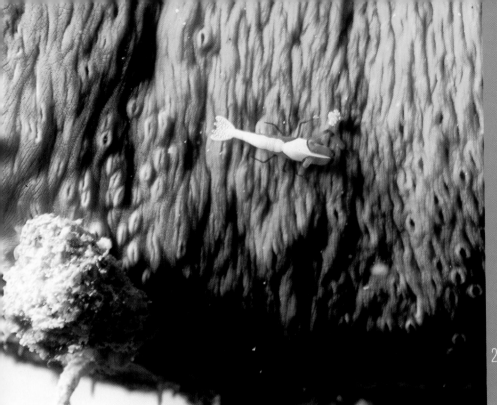

can drop to 5 to 8 metres from November to February. Dives around the park are generally no deeper than 18 to 23 metres. Although there are not many currents to speak of, the occasional thermocline can make diving a 'chilling' experience. The calm and shallow conditions that prevail throughout the park's islands are ideal training grounds for novice divers.

In 1996, the diverse population of corals that supported numerous coral species, invertebrates, sponges and crinoids was devastated by a severe storm. Reef structures over extended areas were completely destroyed, especially around Pulau Sulug and Pulau Mamutik, and the corresponding decline of reef fish and other species was significant. Since then, however, marine life has begun to recover with many corals rebuilding and species returning in numbers and density, among them acroporus, soft corals, sponges, fungi,

nudibranchs, lionfish, shrimp, lobsters, anemones, anemonefish and sea horses.

Diverse macro life forms including the rare dragonet, juvenile ghost pipefish, coral shrimps, gobies and blennies are favourites with 'muck divers' while pods of bottle-nose dolphins and the seasonal sightings of whale sharks when the water teems with krill make for exciting encounters for all.

Competent and professionally managed dive centres are located at the resorts dotting the coastline of Kota Kinabalu, the most notable and convenient of which can be found at the Shangri-La's Tanjung Aru Resort. Access to the dive sites in the park takes only about 10 to 15 minutes.

Above: Emperor shrimps (*Periclimenes imperator*) form symbiotic relationships with a variety of plants, including blue coral (*Heliopora coerulea*).

Facing page: Hingebeak shrimps (*Rhynchocinetes durbanensis*) feeding on trapped microscopic food particles

Getting There

Malaysia Airlines (www.malaysiaairlines.com) and AirAsia (www.airasia.com) have daily flights to Kota Kinabalu from Kuala Lumpur and other major cities. The taxi ride from Kota Kinabalu International Airport to Tanjong Aru Beach in Kota Kinabalu city takes about 10 minutes. Tanjong Aru Beach is the departure point for all trips to the dive sites around Tunku Abdul Rahman Marine Park.

Accommodation

There is no accommodation in Tunku Abdul Rahman Marine Park. However, there are plenty of hotels to choose from in the vicinity of Tanjung Aru Beach in Kota Kinabalu.

Shangri-La's Tanjung Aru Resort
Locked Bag 174
88995 Kota Kinabalu, Sabah
Tel: (60) 88 225 800/ (60) 88 241 800
Fax: (60) 88 217 155
Email: tah@shangri-la.com

Hyatt Regency Kinabalu
Jalan Datuk Salleh Sulong
Locked Bag 47
88991 Kota Kinabalu, Sabah
Tel: (60) 88 221 234
Fax: (60) 88 218 909
Email: hyatt@hyattkk.com.my
Website: www.kinabalu.regency.hyatt.com

Casuarina Hotel
Lorong Ikan Lais
Jalan Mat Salleh
Tanjung Aru
88100 Kota Kinabalu, Sabah
Tel: (60) 88 221 000
Fax: (60) 88 223 000
Email: casuarin@tm.net.my
Website: www.casuarinahotel.com

Beverly Hotel
Lorong Kemajuan
88000 Kota Kinabalu, Sabah
Tel: (60) 88 258 998
Fax: (60) 88 258 778

Promenade Hotel
No 4 Lorong Api-Api 3
Api-Api Centre
88000 Kota Kinabalu, Sabah
Tel: (60) 88 265 555
Fax: (60) 88 246 666
Email: enquiry@promenade.com.my
Website: www.promenade.com.my

Diving in Malaysia

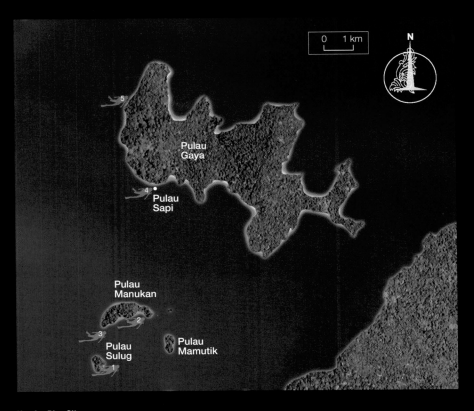

Key for Dive Sites

1: Sulug Reef

2: Manukan Jetty

3: Manukan Reef

4: Keramat Reef

5: Clement Reef

Sulug Reef

Location: 05.57.55N, 115.59.48E

Average depth: 16 m

Maximum depth: 23 m

Dive rating: 🤿 🤿 🤿

Photo rating: 3, Macro

Unique features: Nudibranchs, frogfish, scorpionfish, morays, cleaner shrimps

Hazards: None

Descending initially to around 12 metres on the gradually sloping fringing reef, you will be greeted by the disappointing sight of a barren sandy bottom strewn with coral rubble and palm tree trunks. However, if you continue the descent and head to the right in a southeasterly direction, the seascape transforms into a multitude of mushroom corals, sea whips, blue and green sea stars, featherstars, cushion stars, vase sponges, barrel sponges and Christmas tree worms. Vividly coloured nudibranchs, flatworms and cleaner and coral shrimps clinging to the sea whips can also be seen. Pay attention to the sponges on the reef slopes; you might miss predatory frogfish blending perfectly with the shape and colouration of the sponges, which they use for their stakeouts. Spotted-faced morays peeking out of crevices and gaps eye the passing shoals of cardinalfish, snappers and fusiliers as potential quick meals. The sandy bottom also camouflages scorpionfish, devil fish and crocodile fish. Continuing to the right and gradually ascending, the upper reef is characterised by patches of *Acropora* coral.

1: A painted anglerfish (*Antennarius pictus*) imitates its surroundings while waiting to ambush unwary prey.

2: A banded blenny (*Salarias fasciatus*)

3: A crocodile fish (*Cymbacephalus beauforti*)

4: Spotfin lionfish (*Pterois antennata*) have venomous spines and a painful sting.

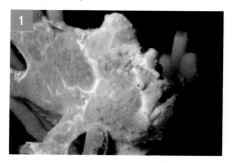

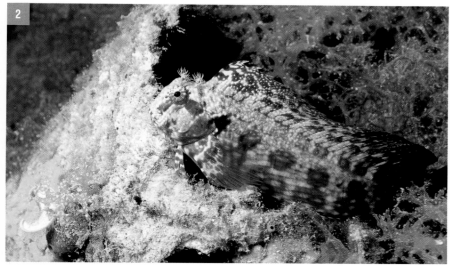

Manukan Jetty

Location: Left of Pulau Manukan Jetty

Average depth: 15 m

Maximum depth: 22 m

Dive rating: 🤿 🤿

Photo rating: 4, Macro

Unique features: Sand divers, dragonets, ghost pipefish, scorpionfish, clownfish

Take note: Never enough film

Hazards: None

If you drop off the jetty, descend to around 18 metres and head left, you will reach a barren slope. This is the result of the storm that swept the area in 1996. However, don't think that diving this site is a waste of time and good air. If you keep still and maintain good buoyancy control, you will see sand divers and unusual multicoloured dragonets appear from under the sandy slope, darting a short distance before burying themselves again at the slightest disturbance.

If you swim for another 30 metres, you will come across some disused fish traps that have become an artificial reef. This artificial reef is a haven for juvenile ghost pipefish, scorpionfish, nudibranchs, anemone clownfish and crocodile fish.

It is strongly advised to dive this site with a buddy only as too many divers will cause visibility to deteriorate quickly if the fine sand is stirred up.

Manukan Reef

Location: Eastern tip of Pulau Manukan Reef

Average depth: 15 m

Maximum depth: 22 m

Dive rating: 🤿 🤿 🤿

Photo rating: 3, Macro

Unique features: Dense growth of staghorn, table and lettuce corals, sea snakes, turtles, barracudas

Hazards: None

This reef slopes to around 22 metres before tapering off to the sandy bottom. The slope is densely covered by terrace-like staghorn, table, lettuce and brain corals, all of which are in full bloom and richly coloured. These corals provide a nutrient-rich habitat for Christmas tree worms, sea stars, featherstars and nudibranchs. If in luck, you may catch a glimpse of a blue-banded sea snake gracefully winding its way through the coral outcrops. This site is a rich hunting ground for scorpionfish and lionfish among the shoals of parrotfish, snappers, fusiliers and catfish. It is not uncommon to see green turtles, jacks and barracudas mingling with the multitude of reef inhabitants.

Other notable dive sites

Keramat Reef is located on the southwestern edge of Pulau Sapi and has a depth of 15 to 22 metres. It has some nice hard coral structures, reef fish, turtles, barracudas and sometimes an octopus. This site is easy to dive.

Clement Reef is west-northwest of Pulau Gaya and has a depth of 15 to 23 metres. Marine life found at this site include large table staghorn, lettuce and brain corals, sponges, Christmas tree worms, cuttlefish, groupers, catfish, lionfish, scorpionfish and stonefish.

1: A highly venomous banded sea snake (*Laticauda colubrina*) on the hunt for prey, usually gobies

2: A green sea turtle (*Chelonia mydas*) settling down for a snooze

LAYANG-LAYANG ATOLL

Coordinates: 07.22.22N, 113.50.48E

Layang-Layang...the name evokes notions of isolation, adventure, walls dropping to a dizzying depth of 2000 metres and pelagic species en masse from schooling hammerhead sharks to serene manta rays. Said to be the marine region with the greatest marine diversity in the world, Terumbu Layang-Layang, or Swallow Reef, is located 300 kilometres to the northwest of Kota Kinabalu in one of the deepest areas of the South China Sea.

The atoll is made up of a ring of 13 reefs. It was artificially made habitable by the Malaysian government in an effort to establish a presence in the resource-rich Spratley Archipelago. The atoll is 8 kilometres by 2 kilometres and accommodates a runway, naval facility and dive resort. The western side of the atoll is home to nesting colonies of brown boobies and great crested, scooty and noody terns.

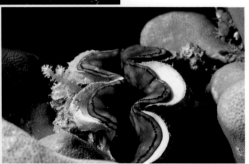

Left: Abundant nutrients carried by the ocean current of Layang-Layang Atoll enable the rich growth of this soft coral (*Siphonogorgia* sp.).

Inset: The giant clam (*Tridacna crocea*) possesses zooxanthellae, microscopic algal cells that produce food for their host.

Diving Layang-Layang Atoll

Diving Layang-Layang is best from March to October but can be year round, although the general perception is that diving during the northeast monsoon is an absolute no-no. Weather patterns in the past years, however, suggest that even during this much-disliked period, diving is entirely feasible and thoroughly enjoyable. Visibility and sea quality may be less than perfect on certain days but usually last only a few hours.

It is important to keep in mind that no two dives—even at the same site—are the same. What you will see is affected by change in currents, weather and time of day. Consequently, each dive will offer a different experience. On one dive, you may see manta rays, hammerheads, green turtles and reef sharks at a cleaning station; on the next, schools of jacks and barracudas. Although you should not expect blue waters and visibility of 50 metres on every dive, the remoteness and people's awareness of the environment while developing the area have helped the reefs remain in pristine condition.

There are two distinct aspects to diving in Layang–Layang and exploring its rich biodiversity. First, the vertical walls that descend to a dizzying depth of about 2000 metres are populated by pelagic species and gravity-defying gorgonian fans. Second, the shallower reef plateaus and ledges of the reef around 15 metres are home to a multitude of reef fish, corals, crustaceans and the tiniest of macro life forms. It is not uncommon to encounter schools of dolphins playing in the wake of the boat and, during certain months, migrating whale sharks. The distance from the continental shelf almost guarantees excellent horizontal visibility for every dive.

Due to this exceptional horizontal visibility, it is very easy to exceed maximum safe diving depths or accumulate decompression time. Exceeding 40 metres or not observing non-decompression time limits (the use of a dive computer is highly recommended) will earn you a warning. A second violation will mean you will not be permitted to dive again. The dive boats are comfortable and spacious purpose-built twin-engine catamarans.

It might be necessary at this point to dispel the common misconception that diving in Layang-Layang is only for the advanced or experienced diver. Every certified diver, and that includes entry-level open water certification, is perfectly safe to dive here within the limits of the training received.

Facing page: Scalloped hammerhead sharks (*Sphyrna lewini*), although solitary, often form migratory schools that cruise the reefs of Layang-Layang near deep drop-offs.

Below: The steep walls and swift currents provide the perfect environs for magnificent gorgonian fans (*Subergorgia mollis*).

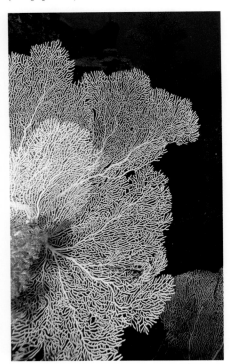

Getting There

Flying AirAsia (www.airasia.com) direct from Kuala Lumpur International Airport to Kota Kinabalu is the most convenient and cost-effective option. If you travel with Malaysia Airlines (www.malaysiaairlines.com), you will need to transfer from the international terminal at Kota Kinabalu Airport to the old terminal (and with all the dive gear weighing you down, this may seem the less attractive option). Direct international flights to Kota Kinabalu are also available. From Kota Kinabalu, a private charter company flies to Pulau Layang-Layang. Flights are arranged by Layang Layang Island Resort and take about 1 hour.

Accommodation

Layang Layang Island Resort
Main Office: A-0-3 Block A, Ground Floor
Megan Phileo Avenue II
12 Jalan Yap Kwan Seng
50450 Kuala Lumpur
Tel: (60) 3 2162 2877
Fax: (60) 3 2162 2980
Email: layang@pop.jaring.my
Website: www.layanglayang.com

D
i
v
i
n
g

i
n

M
a
l
a
y
s
i
a

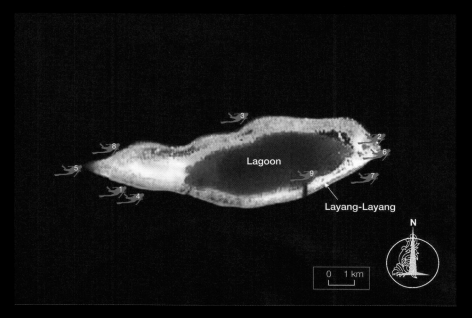

Lagoon

Layang-Layang

N

0 1 km

Key for Dive Sites

1: Shark's Cave
2: Gorgonian Forest
3: Crack Reef

4: D'Wall
5: The Valley
6: The Point

7: Dogtooth Lair
8: Wrasse Strip
9: House Reef

Shark's Cave

Location: Southeastern tip of the atoll

Average depth: 20 m

Maximum depth: 40 m

Dive rating: 🐬 🐬 🐬 🐬

Photo rating: 4, Wide angle

Unique features: Gorgonians, cave, leopard sharks, nurse sharks, white-tip sharks, rays

Hazards: Generally none but monitor bottom line

Leaving the lagoon through the new channel, the entry point of Shark's Cave, one of the most sought-after dive spots in Layang-Layang, is a 15-minute boat ride to the southeastern tip of the atoll.

Descend to a depth of around 26 metres and keep the wall to your right. A sandy ledge interrupts the seemingly endless continuity of the wall as you pass large colourful gorgonian fans, tube corals and a variety of reef fish darting up and down. The sandy patch is a preferred resting place for leopard sharks and stingrays. At the end of the ledge appears the main attraction of this site—the shark's cave.

The cave is a sandy recess in the wall about 15 metres wide and 3 metres high. The back of the cave narrows to 1.5 metres. Quite often, groups of white-tip sharks and leopard sharks can be seen huddling together. These sharks can be approached but it is advisable to avoid blocking the entrance or approaching the sharks from the front as this may agitate them, something you definitely do not want to do. Spotted eagle and grey stingrays are also not uncommon, favouring to rest at the sandy entrance of the cave.

Ascending to the shallower part of the reef, a school of bumphead parrotfish, the occasional napoleon wrasse, jacks, giant groupers and the usual assortment of triggerfish, batfish and emperorfish mingle among the rich soft and hard corals.

This is an easy dive but is seasonally dependent. At the end of July, typhoons in the South China Sea cause waves up to 3 metres high and sub-surface swells. This makes exit and entry into the dive boat challenging for the less-experienced diver.

1: Rich growth of sponges (*Petrosiidae* sp.) and gorgonians

2: A spectacular view from inside Shark's Cave into the expanse of Layang-Layang Atoll

3: A harlequin sweetlip (*Plectorhinchus chaetodonoides*)

Gorgonian Forest

Location: Eastern side of the atoll

Average depth: 25 m

Maximum depth: 40 m

Dive rating: 🤿 🤿 🤿

Photo rating: 4, Wide angle

Unique features: Abundance of gorgonians, barracudas, hammerheads, bumphead parrotfish

Hazards: Current; don't venture too far from the wall

The Gorgonian Forest, adjacent to The Point and Dogtooth Lair, is one of the premium dive sites in Layang-Layang. You can reach it in 15 minutes by boat via the new channel. Descending to a depth of 35 metres, the wall is alive with a forest-like abundance of large, healthy gorgonians fans, polyps feeding in the passing current, scarlet whip corals and barrel sponges.

1: Lush soft coral (*Sarcophyton* sp.)

2: Although nocturnal, lattice soldierfish (*Myripristis violacea*) are often seen in caves and under large overhangs during the day.

3: Porcelain crabs (*Neopetrolisthes ohshimai*) are often found living in anemones and corals.

Swimming away from the wall and looking into the deep blue expanse of the open sea, schools of big-eyed jacks, lone barracudas and flashes of scalloped hammerhead sharks, either solitary, swimming close to the reef or in a school, cruise off the wall into the open water usually against the flow of the current. Some advice to underwater photographers: These animals are easily frightened, especially if you use a flash. Therefore, it is best to photograph using available light, pointing the camera towards the surface and capturing their silhouettes in the blue water.

Ascending to the upper portion of the reef to about 15 to 20 metres, sizeable schools of wrasses, batfish, surgeonfish, great barracudas and smaller groups of or single bumphead parrotfish complement the richness and diversity of the reef. Ribbon eels can be encountered at the sandy regions of the plateau and don't be surprised to see napoleon wrasses and schools of big-eye trevallies. Keep a lookout for the shy yet approachable moray eels which hide inside crevices and curiously investigate the bubble-blowing visitors.

Crack Reef

Location: Northern side of the atoll

Average depth: 20–25 m

Maximum depth: 35 m

Dive rating: 🤿 🤿 🤿 🤿

Photo rating: 4, Wide angle; 4, Macro

Unique features: Turtles, white-tip sharks, triggerfish, nudibranchs

Hazards: None

Crack Reef is the furthest away site from the dive centre. It takes 30 minutes by boat to get there, riding through the old channel and passing the bird sanctuary before turning to the northern side of the atoll.

Descending along a crack in the wall (hence the name 'Crack Reef') to a depth of 35 metres, formations of sea fans and densely growing hard and soft corals are habitats for a variety of reef fish and crustaceans while sharks and turtles lazily drift. Occasionally, schools of bumphead parrotfish cruise the reef just below the surface and a number of titan and clown triggerfish forever guard their nesting areas during the mating season. It is good practice to stay well clear of these protective and aggressive species. In the cracks and crevices of the boulders and branches of the acroporus, hordes of cleaner shrimps, nudibranchs, snails, flatworms and gobies can be seen foraging for food.

Crack Reef is a wonderful site to explore at a leisurely pace. It allows you to stay in the shallow depths and concentrate on the smaller but equally fascinating species that so often get ignored when faced with the vast numbers of pelagic species in Layang-Layang.

D' Wall

Location: Southwestern side of the atoll

Average depth: 20 m

Maximum depth: 40 m

Dive rating: 🤿 🤿 🤿 🤿 🤿

Photo rating: 5, Wide angle

Unique features: Breathtaking wall, gorgonians, sharks, shoals of jacks and bumphead parrotfish

Hazards: Watch your depth!

As its name implies, D'Wall drops 2000 metres into the darkness of the ocean. The wall is adorned with large gorgonians, lush sponges, sea whips, tube corals and ever-present featherstars. Shoals of jacks, surgeonfish, snappers, batfish and small reef fish seem to cascade down the wall. White-tip, grey reef and hammerhead sharks and the occasional manta ray cruise the area while triggerfish, green turtles and a lone napoleon wrasse move along the edge of the wall.

Depending on the time of day and direction of the sunlight (the afternoon seems best), the upper reef, just below the surface where the waves break over Layang-Layang Atoll, is magnificent with its hard and soft corals accompanied by juvenile reef fish such as batfish, angelfish, moray eels and schools of bumphead parrotfish. Compared to the northern and western sides of the atoll, this is an easy dive due to calmer waters.

1: A manta ray (*Manta brevirostris*) cruising the depths of Layang-Layang Atoll

2: Schooling cardinalfish (*Apogonidae*)

Facing page: Diving along D'Wall–a breathtaking drop into the depths of Layang-Layang Atoll

The Valley

Location: 15 minutes via new channel on western side of the atoll

Average depth: 15 m

Maximum depth: 20 m

Dive rating: 🤿 🤿 🤿

Photo rating: 4, Macro

Unique features: Garden eels, ribbon eels, anemones, sweetlips, nudibranchs

Hazards: Nasty titan triggerfish when nesting

The exciting feature of this site is the sandy bottom itself. Here, there are scores of garden eels swaying with the passing current, colourful ribbon eels beating a hasty retreat when approached too closely, gobies peeking out of the burrows that they share with crayfish and clown anemonefish in symbiotic relationship with sea anemones. Curious moray eels will also investigate you for nutritional purposes. Various species of triggerfish seem to have a propensity to nest on the sandy area of the valley and are not to be messed with. Leave the area should you attract their attention.

A gently sloping sandy area, the Valley is punctuated by occasional rocks and hard corals descending to about 15 metres before steeply dropping away into the abyss of Layang-Layang. If you are expecting to see pelagic species, it will appear, at first sight, to be a rather desolate area with little to catch your attention. However, the sandy area and coral outcrops are teeming with squirrelfish, butterflyfish, black-spotted pufferfish, spotted sweetlips, colourful crustaceans, nudibranchs, flatworms and cleaning stations for the multitude of reef inhabitants.

Right: The pristine upper region of a reef in Layang-Layang Atoll

The Point

Location: 07.43.63N, 113.91.4E

Average depth: 25 m

Maximum depth: 35 m

Dive Rating: 🤿 🤿 🤿 🤿

Photo Rating: 4, Wide angle

Unique Features: Plenty of reef sharks off the wall

Hazards: None

Descending initially to 30 metres, white-tip, grey reef and scalloped hammerhead sharks are commonplace here. The latter make a slow ascent up the wall into the upper regions of the reef and then majestically disappear into the Layang-Layang abyss. Green turtles, soft corals, featherstars, snappers, trevallies, batfish, triggerfish, numerous schools of small reef fish and gorgonian fans populate the upper part of the wall and the reef. At about 15 metres, a lone napoleon wrasse has been known to move along the edge of the wall. The upper reef is magnificent with its hard and soft corals. It is an easy dive in calmer waters as compared to the western side of the island. If you keep the wall to your right, you will end your dive near Dogtooth Lair. Keeping the wall to your left will bring you to Gorgonian Forest.

Dogtooth Lair

Location: Eastern side of the atoll; the dive starts at the end of the runway

Average depth: 15 m

Maximum depth: 25 m

Dive rating: 🤿 🤿 🤿 🤿

Photo rating: 4, Wide angle

Unique features: Dogtooth tuna, shoals of jacks, hammerhead sharks, gorgonians

Hazards: Sometimes strong currents

Divers descend to around 25 metres in the sometimes strong, nutrient-rich current along the wall. The site is richly populated by large gorgonians and sea fans and packs of fierce-looking dogtooth tuna that cruise along the drop-off. Shoals of jacks, surgeonfish and fusiliers mingle with turtles gliding by. Due to the stronger currents, hammerhead sharks are encountered quite often. The wall has plenty of ledges and overhangs to explore with pufferfish, leaffish and stingrays either resting or getting 'serviced' at cleaning stations. Shoals of small reef fish mingle among the brain and soft corals at the top of the reef.

Wrasse Strip

Location: 20 minutes; northwestern side of the atoll

Average depth: 20 m

Maximum depth: 25 m

Dive rating: 🤿 🤿 🤿 🤿

Photo rating: 4, Wide angle

Unique features: Mantas, hammerheads, rich coral reef

Hazards: None

Gradually sloping to a depth of around 25 metres before dropping into the fathomless depth of the sea, Wrasse Strip is an extremely rich coral reef.

House Reef

Location: 07.22.22N, 113.50.48E

Average depth: 5 m

Maximum depth: 8 m

Dive rating:

Photo rating: 4, Macro

Unique features: Nursery of Layang-Layang Atoll

Hazards: None

If you want to see some macro life to round off your last day of diving at Layang-Layang, you should explore the house reef. Starting about 100 metres to the left of the jetty, this site acts as the nursery of the atoll. Between 3 and 8 metres, juvenile groupers, emperorfish, pipefish, gobies, nudibranchs, wrasses and varieties of coral shrimp grow in a safe haven among boulders, cement blocks, metal frames and wooden logs until they mature and venture into the depths of the surrounding sea.

The Mysterious Aerodrome

Some time ago, a report surfaced in a dive magazine about a mysterious dive site called the Aerodrome, the location of which was a closely guarded secret by resident dive masters. The story claimed the site was a huge cave or overhang—large enough to accommodate 3 Boeing 747s—that teemed with pelagic species. Sadly, this appears to be a myth and requests to dive this site will just earn you blank looks from the locals and resident dive masters.

1: Coral (*Acropora cerealis*) in full bloom

2: Black-tail humbugs (*Dascyllus melanurus*) are common in lagoons and congregate among coral outcrops (*Seriatopora hystrix*).

3: A close-up of hard coral (*Acropora cerealis*)

MIRI

Coordinates: 04.24N, 113.52E

Left: Elegant white whip coral (*Ellisella* sp.) is common on the patch reefs of Miri.

Inset: A solitary soft coral (*Echinigorgia* sp.) perched on an outcrop of the reef

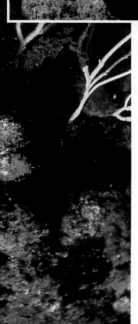

Miri, in many people's mind (and that includes most West Malaysians), is a town that caters to the oil industry and is characterised by offshore oilrigs, oil terminals, busy riverside jetties and little else. Indeed, since the discovery of oil in 1910, this resource-based industry has dominated the life and economy of the town and its surrounding area. However, Miri has developed into a destination that has much more to offer than just oilrigs.

Various long-range infrastructure development programs, including road construction, communication, healthcare and a multitude of other related projects, have been implemented in the last 10 years. The most recent additions are the airport and Asean Bridge. This bridge spans the Baram River which must be crossed on the way to Brunei. Its construction has eliminated the need to rely on the dreaded ferry to cross the river.

Concerted efforts to develop Miri and its surrounding area into a major tourist destination are well under way. Its natural wonders, ranging from national parks and reefs to the Mulu Caves and Bario Highlands, and its rich cultural heritage now attract visitors from across the world. It is also proliferating itself as a centre for education with a number of local and international tertiary institutions offering excellent programs.

Although Miri is rapidly becoming a modern township, it has retained its unique charm and cultural diversity. A visit to the market, where members of native tribes such as the Melanau, Iban, Bidayuh and Kayan sell their products, is an experience not to be missed. Sarawak pineapple, strangely coloured bananas, the famed Sarawak black pepper and the wild growing and oddly curled midin vegetable are items not to be found elsewhere.

Food and eating must be one of the favourite pastimes of the local population and visitors alike. The river front comes alive around sunset when chairs and tables miraculously appear. The freshest catch of seafood and other local delights will surely satisfy even the most discerning gourmet, and all at a fraction of the price that city folk are used to paying.

For eco-tourists and nature lovers, or for those complying with the no-fly requirement after a few days of diving, various nature-oriented tours originate from Miri. The Niah Caves, Loagan Bunut National Park, Limbir Hills National Park, Bario Highlands and the famed Mulu National Park are all within easy distance of the town.

Diving Miri

Normally, the last thing on any scuba diver's mind would be to dive this oilrig-invested coastline, when there is the entire east coast of the peninsula or more exotic locations in Sabah to choose from. However, Miri's coastline, which fronts the South China Sea and forms part of the continental shelf, has a healthy patch reef system that is largely undiscovered and undisturbed by commercial development. According to some marine scientists who have documented this area, the Miri reefs are among the healthiest in Malaysia, housing over 400 species of coral. Efforts by relevant government agencies are underway to zone and designate the area as a marine protected area to accord it much needed protection.

Diving the Miri reefs is dynamic and never boring. One dive may take you into a magical garden of a kaleidoscope of colours and shapes; on the next, schools of jacks, barracudas or teeming macro life will captivate you. Don't expect blue water and unlimited visibility on every dive, but what you will find below the surface is surely one of the most pristine and captivating reefs of Malaysia. I hesitate to describe it as an underwater jungle; rather a garden in perfect balance.

As on the east coast of the peninsula, the best time to dive Miri's reefs is from March to October. The high winds during the northeast monsoon, occasionally reaching 40 to 50 knots, and the generally shallower depth of the reefs result in significant amounts of sediment and suspended solids, increasing the possibility of severely limited visibility.

As dives are typically organised as day trips by the dive operators, 2 to 3 boat dives per trip are the norm. Pre-dive briefings are comprehensive and place emphasis on safety and good dive practices, i.e. look but don't touch. Rental equipment and well-maintained tanks that are always filled with more than enough air make dive preparations hassle free. If obtaining an advanced certificate or just learning to dive is your calling, the dive operators offer a full range of PADI programs.

The comfortable, purpose built twin-engine dive boats normally leave from the riverside jetty in the centre of bustling Miri town. Being picked up from any hotel in town is normally part of the package offered by the operator.

Once under way, the boat cruises past oilrigs, supply vessels and the occasional dead crocodile on the riverbank (putting a damper on any notion to dive in the river). All of the more than dozen charted dive sites are located 10 to 30 kilometres southwest of Miri town and can be reached within 15 to 45 minutes. The sea is usually calm and experiences hardly any current, making for very relaxed and easy dives. Most of the hazards arise from not monitoring bottom time.

As there are no permanent buoys set at the charted sites, descending and ascending, including the safety stops, are done with the aid of the anchor line. Unfortunately, dropping the anchor sometimes causes damage to the corals.

1: Lush soft corals (*Dendronephthya* sp.) and a sea fan (*Paracis* sp.)

2: Sea anemone (*Stichodactyla haddoni*) and whip corals (*Ellisella* sp.)

Getting There

Both Malaysia Airlines (www.malaysiaairlines.com) and AirAsia (www.airasia.com) operate daily direct flights to Miri. The transfer from Miri Airport to town takes 10 to 15 minutes by either bus or taxi.

Accommodation

Miri offers accommodation for every budget, from very comfortable and affordable hotels to small budget hotels in the centre of town.

Park City Everly Hotel
Jalan Temenggong, Datuk Oyong Lawai
98008 Miri, Sarawak
Tel: (60) 85 418 888
Fax: (60) 85 419 999
Email: reservation.pehm@vhmis.com

Rihga Royal Hotel Miri
Jalan Temenggong Datuk Oyong Lawai
98008 Miri, Sarawak
Tel: (60) 85 421 121
Fax: (60) 85 421 099
Email: reservation@righamiri.com
Website: www.rihgamiri.com/

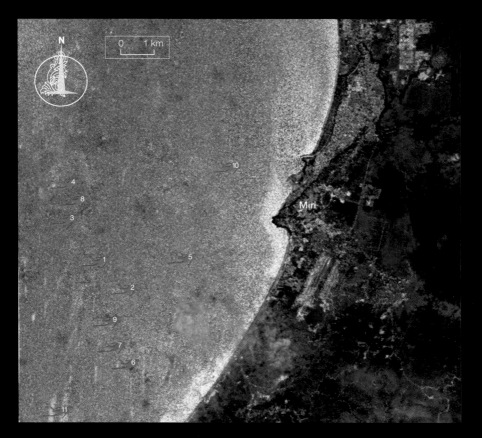

Key for Dive Sites

1: Batu Belais Reef	5: Eve's Garden	9: Sunday Reef
2: Anemone Garden	6: Siwa North	10: Atago Maru
3: Barracuda Point	7: Siwa, or Adam's, Valley	11: Sri Gadong Wreck
4: Tukau Drop-Off	8: Santak Point	

Batu Belais Reef

Location: 04.19.368 N, 113.49.338 E

Average depth: 15 m

Maximum depth: 17 m

Dive rating: 🤿 🤿 🤿

Photo rating: 4, Wide angle

Unique features: Diverse range of healthy gorgonians and sea fans

Hazards: None

Batu Belais Reef is considered the premium site of the Miri patch reef system and can be reached in around 20 minutes from the town jetty. Descend along the buoy line to what is essentially a flat bottom with a sprinkling of small- to medium-sized boulders at around 15 metres. Here you will see a breathtaking abundance of gorgonians in all shapes and colours (some spanning almost 2 metres), white whip corals and lush soft and encrusting corals among medium-sized boulders. The usually good horizontal visibility will reveal what could best be described as a serene, beautiful garden in full bloom. Schools of yellow snappers, jacks, angelfish, lizardfish, multicoloured nudibranchs and butterflyfish create a picture of nature in balance. Batfish are ever present. Good buoyancy control is advisable in order not to break any of the fragile gorgonians or sea fans. This is a site that should definitely be dived more than once.

1 & 3: Whip corals (*Ellisella* sp.) in breathtaking colours

2: A dive-thru decorated with soft corals (*Dendronephthya* sp.) in the clear waters of Miri's reefs–a feature popular with divers

Anemone Garden

Location: 04.17.535N, 113.49.550E

Average depth: 10 m

Maximum depth: 15 m

Dive rating: 🐟 🐟 🐟

Photo rating: 3, Macro

Unique features: Carpet-like pink anemones, teeming macro life

Hazards: None

Located to the southwest of the jetty, this site is aptly named after the carpet-like pink anemones that cover most of the reef at a depth of 10 to 15 metres and their perennial tenants—the clownfish. Large boulder formations, some of which reach 2 to 3 metres in height, are interspersed throughout the site. These formations are densely populated by tube worms that beat a hasty retreat when you get too close.

This site is a feast for the eye for macro life enthusiasts, with its bubble corals, staghorn corals, soft corals, featherstars and rich diversity of reef fish. Mantis shrimps, nudibranchs, schooling yellowtails and giant clams are all found in significant numbers. The patient diver will even be treated to a manicure by one of the site's cleaner shrimps, ever ready and waiting under boulders and crevices.

1: Anemonefish (*Amphiprion clarkia*) usually do not extend their territory beyond their host anemone.

2: A reef in perfect balance—sea anemone with symbiotic clownfish surrounded by ascidian filter feeders

Barracuda Point

Location: 04.20.066N, 113.45.999E

Average depth: 26 m

Maximum depth: 28 m

Dive rating: 🐬 🐬 🐬

Photo rating: 3, Wide angle

Unique features: School of great barracudas

Hazards: Exceeding bottom time

This is one of the furthest away sites from the jetty and can be reached in about 45 minutes. Descending to 26 metres, the seabed topography is essentially flat with some hard corals and boulders. Whip corals and schools of yellow snappers, angelfish and emperorfish break the monotony of an otherwise barren seascape.

Some might be a little sceptical as to whether barracudas will be encountered here as the name of a dive site does not necessarily mean you will see what the name suggests. However, direct your attention to the surface where sleek, silvery bodies might materialise. A school of 300 to 400 great barracudas, which usually seems to stay at around 15 metres, often descends to pay a visit. Check with the resident dive masters to find out the best times to dive this site.

1: A school of chevron barracudas (*Sphyraena putnamiae*) in perfect formation

2: A picture-perfect congregation of sea stars (*Linckia laevigata*), soft corals (*Dendronephthya* sp.) and whip corals (*Ellisella* sp.)

2

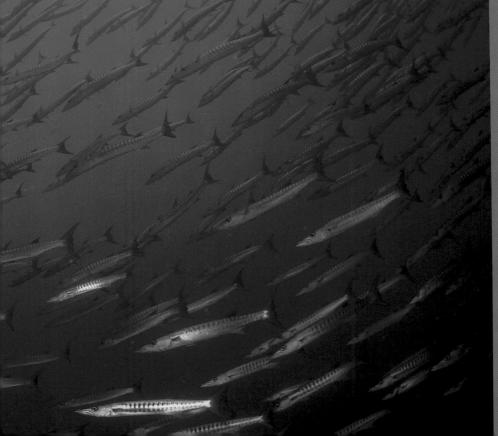

1: An arrangement of soft corals and sea fans

2: A school of yellow-band fusiliers (*Pterocaesio chrysozona*) and black-spot snappers (*Lutjanus fulviflamma*) heading into the lower regions of the reef

Tukau Drop-Off

Location: 04.24.143N, 113.44.532E

Average depth: 26 m

Maximum depth: 40 m

Dive rating: 🐋 🐋 🐋

Photo rating: 3, Wide angle

Unique features: Nurse sharks, leopard sharks, boulders, hard corals

Hazards: Exceeding bottom time

Near the looming platforms of Tukau oilrig is Tukau Drop-Off, one of the sites furthest from the coast. Reaching a depth of 26 metres on the initial descent, the wall that delineates this site quickly drops to 40 to 50 metres. The seabed is largely a sandy bottom with hard corals and boulders that are home to lone barracudas and occasional leopard and nurse sharks. Large schools of yellow snappers forever on the move, nudibranchs, damselfish and angelfish characterise this site. It is good practice to carefully monitor bottom time (normally around 20 to 25 minutes) as the entire dive is between 26 and 28 metres.

Eve's Garden

Location: 04.19.335N, 113.50.102E

Average depth: 7 m

Maximum depth: 12 m

Dive rating: 🤿 🤿 🤿

Photo rating: 3, Macro

Unique features: Nudibranchs, juvenile stonefish, sponges

Hazards: None

For those divers who have an affinity to explore macro life, Eve's Garden, which is 15 minutes from the jetty, will make for an interesting and relaxed dive. At a depth between 5 and 12 metres, a teeming nursery of reef fish abounds among large rock boulders, soft corals, sponges and whip corals. From juvenile groupers, emperorfish, stonefish, scorpionfish, pipefish, nudibranchs, gobies and wrasses to shrimps, the patient observer will discover a teeming and captivating marine environment.

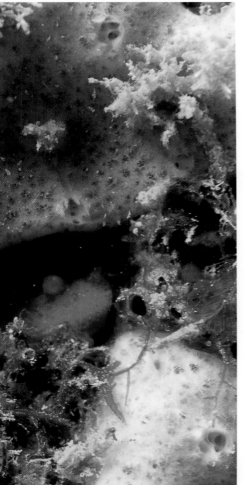

1: A Lance blenny (*Aspidontus dussumieri*) taking refuge among sponges

2: A solitary ascidian (*Polycarpa aurata*)

Other notable dive sites

Siwa North (04.15.596 N, 113.49.016 E) is where, at the right time, leopard sharks and occasional manta rays can be encountered.

Siwa, or **Adam's Valley** (04.16.437N, 113.48.940E) and **Santak Point** (04.24.143N, 113.44.695E) feature amazing sea fan gardens, a wide variety of large gorgonians and whip corals.

Sunday Reef (04.17.210N, 113.49.181E) is where moray eels and stonefish can regularly be seen among boulders populated with featherstars and Christmas trees in vivid colours.

Atago Maru (04.28.40N, 113.57.38E) and **Sri Gadong Wreck** (04.08.32N, 113.43.11E) are home to schools of groupers and jacks.

SHIPWRECK DIVING

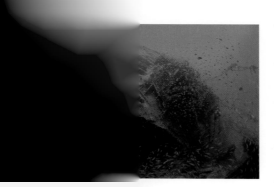

Left: Divers performing a mandatory safety stop in the deep blue expanse of the South China Sea

Inset: Remnants of the Rice Bowl wreck, a Japanese freighter purportedly sunk during the Pacific War

The Malaysian seas, notably the regions around Pulau Tioman, Pulau Aur and Pulau Labuan, are home to numerous shipwrecks. Some of these shipwrecks bore witness to fierce battles or great tragedies while others are the result of infringements of maritime or fishing zone restrictions. Due to the relative shallowness of the South China Sea, many of these wrecks are accessible to recreational divers and are home to a rich diversity of marine life.

As there are many small wrecks located throughout the coastal zones of the peninsula and around Malaysia's islands, only major and/or historically significant wrecks are listed here.

Shipwrecks around Pulau Tioman

Popular with advanced technical divers, the wrecks of the British Royal Navy warships HMS *Prince of Wales* and HMS *Repulse* are 68 kilometres north-northeast of Pulau Tioman, off the east coast of the peninsula. They are both listed as 'protected places' under the classification of British war graves. This means that under British law divers cannot penetrate the wrecks or remove any artefacts from them. In essence, it is legal to dive the wrecks as long as they are dived respectfully.

HMS *Prince of Wales*

Location: 03.34N, 104.26E; northeast of Pulau Tioman

Average depth: 46 m

Maximum depth: 80 m

Hazards: Only advanced technical divers may dive the wreck

On 10 December 1941, during the Pacific War, HMS *Prince of Wales* was attacked by Japanese high-level bombers and torpedo planes. The warship was struck by two to three torpedoes on her port side, four torpedoes on her starboard side and one bomb on her catapult deck. She subsequently sank.

HMS *Prince of Wales* is almost completely capsized, with her shallowest part, the starboard bilge keel, at 46 metres. Visibility of the wreck is generally 15 metres but can be less than 3 metres in the currents that are usually present.

HMS *Repulse*

Location: 03.45N, 104.24E

Average depth: 54 m

Maximum depth: 85 m

Hazards: Only advanced technical divers may dive the wreck

On 10 December 1941, during the Pacific War, HMS *Repulse* was attacked by Japanese high-level bombers and torpedo planes. The warship was damaged by five torpedoes and one bomb strike and consequently sank. Visibility is sometimes so good that the wreck can be seen from the surface through a face mask, even though the stern is at a depth of 58 metres. The wreck is capsized to port.

Other notable shipwrecks around Pulau Tioman

The following wrecks are best dived during a live-on-board excursion due to their distance from the mainland and islands.

Rompin Wreck (Kapal Rompin), 02.57.76N,103.44.33E; depth 25–28 m. This cargo ship has good coral growth, reef fish and macro life such as nudibranchs and coral shrimps.

Timor Wreck (Kapal Timor), 02.55.94N,103.44.62E; depth 24–29 m. The deck of this cargo ship is carpeted with small colourful soft corals, juvenile reef fish, pufferfish and nurse sharks.

Berhala Wreck, 03.43.19N, 103.48.69E; depth 16–19 m. This 50-metre long Japanese anti-aircraft boat has well-preserved twin-barrel guns aft and fore and ammunition litters the seabed. Shoals of reef fish populate the area. It is a nice wreck to photograph if the conditions are right.

1: Encrusting corals cover the anti-ship guns of the
   Berhala wreck.

2: Soft corals (*Dendronephthya* sp.) cover the structures of
   the Rompin wreck.

3: Wrecks are perfect artificial reefs, providing a habitat for
   rich marine life.

Shipwrecks around Pulau Labuan

The duty-free Federal Territory of Pulau Labuan is situated off the coast of northwestern Borneo and is surrounded by six small, picturesque islands. The island's strategic location means that it is within close proximity to major shipping routes.

Four shipwrecks, all of which rest at depths of 30 to 35 metres, can be explored around the waters of Pulau Labuan: two from World War II and two from the 1980s. Visibility ranges from 5 to 20 metres. The types of diving skill required for these wrecks are rated from novice to experienced wreck diving, with penetration into the hulls. The Blue Water, American and Australian wrecks should only be dived by experienced divers. Descent to the wrecks is via an anchor line that is set just prior to the dive. During tidal movements, some surface currents are present which dissipate as you descend.

American Wreck (USS Salute)

Location: Southwest of Pulau Rusukan Besar

Average depth: 21 m

Maximum depth: 33 m

Dive rating: 🐳 🐳 🐳

Photo rating: 3, Wide angle

Unique features: Sponges, shoals of batfish, sweetlips, lionfish, scorpionfish

Hazards: Exceeding bottom time; surface currents

The USS *Salute,* an American minehunter, was serving in the Philippines during the Pacific War when she struck a mine and sank in June 1945.

The 60-metre long wreck, which buckled and folded back on herself when she sank, is a tangled mass of metal and cables. The wreck and its surrounding seabed are littered with ammunition shells, shoes, cutlery and bottles. There are few corals to explore with the exception of some scattered sponges and soft corals. Shoals of sweetlips, curious batfish, fusiliers and anglefish populate the wreck. Lionfish, scorpionfish and moray eels can be found among metal pieces and broken hull sections. Only experienced wreck divers should attempt to penetrate the hull. In addition, good buoyancy control should be exercised to stay away from the numerous sea urchins.

Australian Wreck (SS *De Klerk/Imabari Maru*)

Location: Southwest of Pulau Rusukan Besar

Average depth: 21 m

Maximum depth: 33 m

Dive rating: 🐳 🐳 🐳

Photo rating: 3, Wide angle

Unique features: Black corals, black-tip reef sharks, jacks, barracudas, frogfish, scorpionfish

Hazards: Exceeding bottom time

A Dutch freight and passenger steamship, the SS *De Klerk* was scuttled in 1942 to prevent it from falling into Japanese hands during the Pacific War. However, the ship was refloated by the Japanese, renamed *Imabari Maru* and used as a cargo ship until she struck a mine and sank en route from Singapore to Manila in September 1944.

Resting on her port side, the vessel, which is 85 metres long with the shallowest depth at 21 metres, is now a rich artificial reef hosting an abundance of marine life. The remaining steel superstructure is covered with black coral trees, featherstars, sea whips, soft corals and stinging hydroids. As is common in these waters, groupers, barracudas, snappers, jacks and small black-tip sharks scout the wreck. The bottom-dwelling and well-camouflaged scorpionfish and stonefish should remind you not to get too close to the wreck. Only those with experience in wreck diving should explore the interior.

Cement Wreck (*Tung Hwuang*)

Location: East of Pulau Kuraman; 21 km from Pulau Labuan

Average depth: 19 m

Maximum depth: 30 m

Dive rating: 🦅 🦅 🦅

Photo rating: 4, Wide angle

Unique features: Black corals, black-tip reef sharks, jacks, barracudas, scorpionfish, frogfish

Hazards: Exceeding bottom time

This freighter was carrying a cargo of cement when it sank off Pulua Labuan. The ship, 92 metres in length and probably the most photogenic of the Labuan wrecks, is in an upright position on the sandy bottom. The top of the wheelhouse is located at 13 metres and the main deck at 18 metres. The wreck is covered in a myriad of soft corals and shoals of batfish, barracudas, yellowtail snappers and fusiliers loiter around it. The cargo holds have become a shelter to green turtles, lionfish, pipefish,

moray eels, damselfish, gobies, cardinalfish and nudibranchs. Moving away from the wreck, you will frequently encounter white-tip reef sharks, rainbow runners and the occasional stingray.

The position of the wreck makes it ideal for novice divers and wreck diving training.

Blue Water Wreck (*Mabini Padre*)

Location: Northeast of Pulau Kuraman; 34 km from Pulau Labuan

Average depth: 25 m

Maximum depth: 35 m

Dive rating: 🦅 🦅 🦅

Photo rating: 3, Wide angle

Unique features: Shoals of reef fish, batfish, snappers, groupers, scorpionfish

Hazards: Surface current; bottom time

The 80-metre long *Mabini Padre* is a Philippine trawler that caught fire and sank in 1981. Lying on her port side, the hull and superstructures are completely intact and make interesting subjects for wreck photography. With the exception of some sponges and algae on the derricks and masts, there is very little coral growth. Shoals of sweetlips, jacks, cardinalfish and fusiliers circulate the wreck while the cargo holds are inhabited by groupers, lionfish and scorpionfish.

Hull penetration should only be attempted by divers with the appropriate experience and training. As with other wrecks lying in these depths, bottom time monitoring is advised. Among the wrecks around Pulau Labuan, this site usually has the best visibility.

Other Sites

Kuantan Wreck

Location: 03.43.19N, 103.48.69E

Average depth: 25 m

Maximum depth: 28 m

Dive rating: 🤿 🤿 🤿

Photo rating: 3, Wide angle

Unique features: Encrusting corals, black-tip reef sharks, stingrays, snappers, barracudas, occasional manta rays

Hazards: Exceeding bottom time

This ship was carrying crude oil when she sank about 32 kilometres off the Malaysian coast. The wreck lies on her port side, from 15 metres below the surface of the water and bottoms at 25 metres. She is about 80 metres long from bow to stern and can easily be circumnavigated in one dive.

The entire wreck is covered with hard and encrusting corals and carpet-like soft corals. Swimming away from the wreck for about 20 to 30 metres and passing an old fish trap, keep a lookout for shoals of jacks, yellow snappers and fusiliers. About half a dozen black-tip reef sharks and stingrays often circle the wreck looking for prey. Batfish in pairs seem to adopt and follow you throughout the dive, only keeping their distance when the black-tips get too close. The deck and surrounding sandy area are populated by soft corals, graceful flatworms, colourful nudibranchs and crustaceans. The wreck also appears to attract manta rays on their migratory path along the east coast of the peninsula. As the depth of the dive is around 25 metres, it is easy to exceed the allowable bottom time. Be careful not to get carried away and overstay.

Rice Bowl Wreck

Location: 06.28N, 116.14E

Average depth: 26 m

Maximum depth: 38 m

Dive rating: 🤿 🤿 🤿

Photo rating: 4, Wide angle

Unique features: Soft corals, sponges, an eagle ray, shoals of snappers and fusiliers

Hazards: Exceeding bottom time

The wreck, resting at a depth of 38 metres, is 150 metres long and believed to be a Japanese freighter that was allegedly sunk during the Pacific War. She is lying on her port side and is in good condition apart from the hole below the waterline that was caused by a torpedo strike. Yellow soft corals, encrusting corals and sponges have grown on the superstructure. Cardinalfish, snappers and fusiliers criss-cross the wreck and a large fishing net snared on the railing. A lone eagle ray can be seen occasionally. The propeller is at a depth of 38 metres and encrusted with colourful hard corals. Kitchen utensils and ammunition litter the holds but only adequately trained divers should attempt penetration.

Due to the very short bottom time, not to mention the size of the wreck, this site should be dived at least twice. The best time to dive is during slack tide when visibility is usually good (20–25 metres). This visibility deteriorates quickly during tidal flows. Descent to the wreck is via an anchor line that also has a spare cylinder and regulator for divers who have exceeded bottom time or been penalised by a lengthy safety stop.

1: The Kuantan wreck teems with rich marine life.

2: Once a trap, this discarded fish cage is now a playground for schools of cardinalfish.

LIVE-ON-BOARD DIVING

Live-on-board diving excursions, or safaris, have become a permanent feature of diving in recent years. These safaris mainly go to the dive destinations off the peninsula; very few ply the waters of the Sulu and Celebes seas. Without doubt, live-on-board diving is a more flexible way of exploring the more remote sites spread off the shores of the South China Sea.

Left: Live-on-board, a more flexible way to explore Malaysia's reefs

Inset: Rows and rows of tanks

The majority of the boats are converted fishing trawlers (20 to 25 metres in length) with varying degrees of comfort and equipment (i.e. echo sounder, GPS, radar, TV etc.). They typically sleep between 12 and 20 divers in air-conditioned twin-share or bunk-type cabins.

The excursions normally last 3 to 5 days and offer excellent value for money as the number of dives is unlimited (but of course within the limits of safe diving practices). The food, three full meals plus snacks, is often local fare with plenty of fresh seafood. A typical day on board a dive boat usually starts with the first dive before breakfast and then follows the cliché of live-on-board diving—dive, eat, sleep, dive, eat, sleep.

During the off-monsoon season (March to October), boats usually depart from the east coast fishing village of Tanjung Gemak, north of Mersing. From November to February, the boats depart from the west coast ports of Kuala Selangor or Lumut. Trips should be booked through one of the various dive shops in Kuala Lumpur.

Below is a list of some of the more notable live-on-board vessels that operate off the peninsula.

Kaleebso, a 23-metre vessel, is manned by 4 crew members. It is equipped with GPS, echo sounder, radar, communication equipment and safety equipment (ranging from oxygen to well-stocked medical supplies). The vessel can comfortably accommodate up to 20 divers in air-conditioned 2- and 3-bed cabins. The upper deck features the dining area and an air-conditioned lounge complete with TV, VCD and reading material. Sufficiently large water tanks mean you will never be deprived of a much-needed shower after a long day of diving. The food is the best I have ever tasted on a dive boat. Supporting the dive operations, the vessel carries an ample supply of tanks and the dive platform is functional and spacious.

Divemaster is a 24–metre converted fishing trawler with modern navigation and communication equipment, such as GPS and depth sounder, an electric compressor and a petrol compressor. It is fully air-conditioned and has comfortable bunk beds for up to 20 people. The two showers are clean and it has flushing toilets. The food is reasonably good and the crew is competent.

My Grace is a 36-metre vessel that has been extensively refitted, modified and updated for regional dive destinations. The boat has 10 air-conditioned twin-share cabins, 4 washrooms, 5 showers, a spacious lounge and dining area fitted with a TV, video recorder, VCD and karaoke system as well as an upper deck for sun bathing. It can comfortably accommodate up to 16 people.

Wavebreaker is a 26-metre converted and refurbished fishing trawler with navigation and communication equipment, such as GPS and a depth sounder. It is fully air-conditioned and has a lounge and comfortable bunk beds for up to 20 divers. The food is reasonably good and the crew is competent.

The following are live-on-board vessels that operate in the Sulu and Celebes seas.

MV Scuba Explorer, a 23-metre vessel, is specially designed for scuba diving cruises. The fully air-conditioned living quarters accommodate up to 14 passengers. On the different decks, divers will find a quadruple shared cabin, four twin cabins and one suite with a double bed. The boat only operates from March to October.

MV Celebes Explorer, a 29-metre vessel with a 7.2-metre beam, is equipped with eight ensuite cabins that have individually controlled air-conditioning, a comfortable lounge with a TV, audio system and mini bar and a spacious sun deck. The meals are buffet style and plentiful. The dive area on board has hot and cold showers as well as storage space for equipment. Dive gear can be rented on a pre-booked basis.

Facing page: The serene Bajau Fishing Village on Pulau Mabul

HYPERBARIC CHAMBERS AND FIRST AID FOR DIVERS

Diving Emergencies

Malaysian Diving Emergency Hotline:

05-930 4114 (24 hours)

The Malaysian Diving Emergency Hotline was set up by the Institute of Underwater and Hyperbaric Medicine and Divers Alert Network (DAN) to facilitate diver evacuation and treatment. The hotline allows divers and doctors to get advice on how to deal with diving illnesses as well as the quickest way to get to a hyperbaric chamber.

Decompression Sickness and Hyperbaric Chambers

Decompression sickness is also known as the bends. It is caused by nitrogen bubbles that form in the bloodstream and tissues of the body. These bubbles occur due to rapid changes in environmental pressure, i.e. if you move too quickly from deep water to shallow water. Symptoms appear soon after the dive has finished and include pain in one or more joints, tingling in the arms or legs, tiredness, weakness and a blotchy rash. Decompression sickness is treated by giving the diver 100 per cent oxygen and placing him or her in a hyperbaric chamber.

It is important to know where the nearest hyperbaric facility is situated in relation to where you are diving. Hyperbaric chambers and treatment facilities can be found at the following locations:

WEST COAST OF PENINSULAR MALAYSIA

Institute of Underwater and Hyperbaric Medicine
Armed Forces Hospital Lumut
RMN Base, 32100 Lumut, Perak
Tel: (60) 5 683 7090 ext 4071
Fax: (60) 5 683 7169
Email: divemed@hatl.gov.my
Website: www.hatl.gov.my/divemed.htm

Centre for Wound Care and Hyperbaric Medicine
16 Persiaran Greentown 1
Greentown Business Centre
30450 Ipoh, Perak
Tel: (60) 5 242 6237
Fax: (60) 5 242 8533
Email: drlee@hbomalaysia.com
Website: www.hbomalaysia.com

EAST COAST OF PENINSULAR MALAYSIA

Kuantan Naval Base
Tg. Gelang
25990 Kuantan, Pahang
Tel: (60) 9 513 3333

For dive sites in Peninsular Malaysia that are located nearer Singapore:

Naval Medicine Hyperbaric Centre
Appointments: (65) 6750 5632
24-Hr Emergency Hotline: (65) 6758 1733
Website: www.mindef.gov.sg/navy/medical/nhc.html

Hyperbaric Medicine Centre
11 Jalan Tan Tock Seng
Basement 1
Singapore 308433
Tel: (65) 6355 9021
Fax: (65) 6250 3995
Email: hbot1@singnet.com.sg

SABAH

c/o Borneo Divers & Sea Sports
9th Floor, Menara Jubili
53 Jalan Gaya
88000 Kota Kinabalu, Sabah
Tel: (60) 88 222 226
Fax: (60) 88 221 550
Email: information@borneodivers.info
Website: www.borneodivers.info

Note: With the move of Sipadan-based operators to nearby Pulau Mabul, this chamber may be decommissioned.

Recompression Chamber Labuan
Pejabat Selam
Markas Wilayah Laut Dua
87007 Labuan, Sabah
Tel: (60) 87 412 122

An additional hyperbaric chamber should be available in the coastal town of Semporna in the near future.

First Aid

If you or a fellow diver is injured during a dive, stop the dive immediately and initiate first aid. You should always seek medical attention.

Seasickness

Seasickness is a disturbance in the balance system of the inner ear. Some people get sick when their eyes are focused on close work, such as donning gear, or when working in an enclosed area. Diesel fumes may also be associated with sickness.

The best treatment for seasickness is to keep your eyes on the horizon, stay on deck and keep yourself well hydrated with non-alcoholic beverages and avoid greasy food. When diving, try to be the first diver in from a heaving boat. Medications that help prevent or alleviate seasickness include Meclizine, Scopolamine, Bonine and Dramamine.

Hazardous Marine Life

Potential hazardous marine life in Malaysia's tropical waters can be divided into the following categories.

Contact Irritants/Toxins

Sponges

Three sponge species, including the red-beard sponge, the fire sponge and the poison-bun sponge, can cause nasty stings and rashes.

Symptoms: Redness, joint pain and swelling

Treatment: Thoroughly rinse the affected area. Apply hydrocortisone ointment to alleviate pain. Infection can develop so see a doctor if the pain persists or the rash spreads.

Sea Anemones and Corals

Sea anemones and corals primarily cause skin abrasions and lacerations that can easily become infected.

Symptoms: Pain, burning sensation and/or itchiness, redness, swelling and increased warmth

Treatment: Thoroughly clean the affected area. Apply topical antibiotics.

Jellyfish and Hydroids

Jellyfish and hydroids like sea wasps and Portuguese Man-of-War have stingers that are able to pierce skin and deliver a painful sting. The sting ranges from mild to severe. Take note: You can also be stung by torn-off tentacles or even when the animal is dead.

Symptoms: Rapid onset of pain, varying from mild to severe, a hot and swollen red rash. Severe stings may cause muscle cramps, abdominal pain, fever, chills, nausea, vomiting, respiratory distress and, in very rare cases, cardiac arrest.

Treatment: Rinse the wound using sea water. Then wash the wound with either alcohol or vinegar. This will deactivate the stinging cells. Remove any tentacles with tweezers. Hydrocortisone cream may be applied 2–3 times daily to help alleviate itching. In serious cases, seek immediate medical attention.

Crown-of-Thorns Starfish

Crown-of-thorns starfish have very sharp spines that can easily break off in wounds. These spines also contain venom, which is released upon contact.

Symptoms: Rapid onset of swelling, redness, severe pain and, with severe reactions, vomiting

Treatment: Remove any loose spines. Do not tug the spines excessively as the tips may break off, leaving the rest of the spine embedded in the wound. Soak the affected area in hot water. Clean the wound thoroughly and administer topical antibiotics.

Sea Urchins

Sea urchins have a globe-shaped body that are covered in spines. These spines contain venom and can cause puncture wounds. Most puncture wounds occur when divers step unsuspectingly on a sea urchin.

Symptoms: Immediate pain, joint pain, swelling and numbness

Treatment: Pull out any protruding spines. The spines are usually so brittle that they will break off in the wound. The body will then either absorb the spine fragments or the fragments will work their way out through the skin. If the spines are embedded near a joint or nerve, see a doctor. Also see a doctor if there are signs of infection. Soaking the wound in hot water (45°–50° Centigrade) for 60–90 minutes will offer relief from the pain and swelling.

Injected Toxins

Cone Shells

These cones possess a stinger that injects venom.

Symptoms: Small puncture wound with localised blanching, pale, bluish colour and swelling. Onset of severe pain, numbness, tingling of the mouth and lips and, in extreme cases, accompanied by muscle paralysis and respiratory distress.

Treatment: Clean the puncture wound with hot water, as hot as the patient can tolerate. Immobilise the affected area and apply a pressure dressing. Do not block circulation.

Make sure that the fingers and toes remain pink. Administer CPR if required. Seek immediate medical attention.

Blue-Ringed Octopus

The small blue-ringed octopus has blue rings and luminous tentacles. The salivary glands of the blue-ringed octopus produce a venom containing tetrodotoxin, which causes paralysis. Most injuries occur when the octopus is stepped on.

Symptoms: The bite is usually painless. Symptoms begin with abnormal sensations of the mouth, neck and head followed by nausea, vomiting, shortness of breath and sometimes lack of respiration. There can be visual disturbances, impaired speech and swallowing, general weakness and paralysis. Symptoms last 4–12 hours.

Treatment: Immobilise the limb, cleanse the affected area and apply a pressure dressing but do not block circulation. Monitor the respiratory functions and administer CPR if necessary. Seek immediate medical attention.

Stingrays

Stingrays have serrated bony spines at the base of their tail. Each spine contains venom. Most injuries occur when you step on a stingray. When you do, it will thrust its tail upwards and inject you with the venom.

Symptoms: Intense pain, local loss of blood supply and swelling around the affected area. The wound is jagged and may contain pieces of spine. Secondary infection is common. Generalised symptoms include salivation, sweating, vomiting, diarrhoea, cramps, low blood pressure and cardiovascular collapse.

Treatment: The treatment is the same as for a sea urchin puncture. Pull out any protruding spines. Spines are usually so brittle that they will break off in the wound. The body will then either absorb the spine fragments or the fragments will work their way out through the skin. If the spines are embedded near a joint or nerve, see a doctor. Also see a doctor if there are signs of infection. Soaking the wound in hot water (45°–50° Centigrade) for 60–90 minutes will offer relief from the pain and swelling.

Scorpionfish

The scorpionfish has venomous spines which produce very painful stings. As it is very good at camouflaging itself, divers can brush against the spines of this fish without even knowing it is there.

Symptoms: Immediate intense pain, redness, swelling and blueness of the skin. Nausea, hypotension, delirium and cardiovascular collapse.

Treatment: Soak the wound in hot water for 30 to 90 minutes to help relieve the pain. Remove any protruding pieces of spine. Clean and dress the affected area. Seek immediate medical attention.

Sea Snakes

The sea snake is an inquisitive but usually non-aggressive creature. Its venom is extremely toxic (2–10 times more poisonous than the king cobra). Many bites are not envenomated. In extreme cases, the bite can be fatal.

Symptoms: Symptoms are often delayed, varying from 10 minutes to 6–8 hours. There is the onset of malaise, anxiety and stiffness, followed by aching and paralysis. Paralysis of the jaw and eyelids are common.

Treatment: Immobilise the affected area and give CPR if needed. Seek immediate medical attention.

Predators

The principal marine predators in Malaysia's waters are barracudas, moray eels and sharks. Actual attacks and fatalities are rare, occurring when a diver is mistaken as a food source or intrudes upon the animal's territory.

Barracudas

Barracudas are bold, inquisitive and fearsome and can be dangerous to humans. The great barracuda is known to have been involved in attacks on swimmers. In reef areas they have been known to inhabit open waters and bay areas in the shadows, under floating objects. They are attracted to shiny, reflective things that look like a possible meal. They cause harm with their sharp jagged teeth and strong tearing jaws.

Moray Eels

Morays enjoy rocky areas and can be found living or just 'hanging out' in holes and crevices and under rocks. To prevent contact and possible severe injury, keep your hands out of rocky areas, holes and crevices. If you must, use a stick to probe. The eels attack with their razor sharp teeth and powerful jaws. Injuries may result in bleeding, severe muscle damage or chipped bones.

Sharks

Sharks do not attack humans for the sole purpose of hunger. In fact, sharks do not know what the feeling of hunger is and can go for many months without feeding. On rare occasions, sharks do attack with the intention of seeking prey.

Sharks may attack humans because they have been provoked. Many spear-fishers have been attacked by reef sharks. This is because when they spear fish, the blood from the fish and subsequent vibrations can result in a feeding frenzy by many sharks. Sharks are attracted by splashing and vibrations in the water, which may also help to explain why they sometimes attach humans.

The following are some measures to help to prevent the possibility of a shark attack.

- If you do see a shark, do not provoke it.

- If you cut or injure yourself, get out of the water immediately. Sharks can smell blood from over a mile away.

- Don't swim in waters that have been deemed dangerous. Avoid swimming in murky waters.

- If you feel something brush up against you, get out of the water to check to make sure that you have not been bitten.

- Watch other fish and turtles in the area. If they start acting erratic, a shark might be in the area.

Treatment: If it is a minor wound, clean it thoroughly and press on it to try to stop the bleeding. Treat for shock, if necessary. If the victim appears pale, sweaty and nauseated, lie him or her down in the recovery position to prevent fainting. Barracudas and sharks can sever arteries and veins, causing rapid blood loss. In such a case, press a towel or anything available directly on the wound. Seek immediate medical attention.

First-Aid Kit for Divers

The following is a suggested list of first-aid supplies that should be available on board a dive boat. As these items are only suggestions, they can be modified according to your needs and level of training.

- Gloves
- Deodorant cleansing soap (antibacterial)
- Household vinegar solution
- Household ammonia
- Antibiotic ointment
- Cortisone cream (1%)
- Non-aspirin pain reliever
- Hot packs
- Cold packs (pain relief)
- Denatured alcohol, 12 oz. bottle (for sterilising instruments)
- Telfa pads or plastic wrap (to cover burns)
- Absorbent dressings (to control severe bleeding with pressure)
- Squeeze bottle of water, 6 oz. (for irrigating eyes and wounds)
- Squeeze bottle of sterile saline
- Sterile cotton, gauze pads and adhesive tape
- Band-Aids and butterfly bandages
- Q-tips
- Tongue depressors
- Disposable cups
- Razor blades (single-edged)
- Shaving cream

- Tweezers or forceps
- Needle nosed pliers with wire cutters (to remove fishhooks)
- Bandage scissors
- Lighter or waterproof matches
- Space blankets
- Backboard, splints and neckbrace
- Penlight
- Seasickness medication
- Pocket mask (eliminates direct contact while resuscitating a person)
- Oxygen is a necessity on any dive boat

None of these items will be of any use if no one on board the boat knows how to administer first aid. All dive masters and instructors should be fully certified in first aid.

The appropriate local emergency information number should be readily available in the boat's first-aid kit. If the kit is used, it should be replenished immediately and updated every 6 months to a year depending on the expiry dates and types of medication it contains.

Note: For purposes of hospital and insurance follow-up, you should keep a record of events in case of an accident while on a dive trip so keep a pen and small notebook handy.

DIGITAL UNDERWATER PHOTOGRAPHY

Underwater photography is a wonderful mechanism for professionals and amateurs alike to showcase their creativity and enthusiasm while documenting the richness and diversity of the Earth's marine ecosystem. What was once the realm of professional photographers, scientists, explorers and wealthy amateurs has, in the past 5 years, become accessible to recreational divers who can now carry affordable digital cameras with them on their diving excursions. As an underwater photographer, my experience with underwater photographic equipment is limited largely to Nikon products.

Digital Photography

The arrival of the digital era has resulted in the corresponding quantum leap in imaging, miniaturisation, affordability, productivity and instant gratification.

Rapid advances in processing power and storage device technology allow for the capture and storage of hundreds of pictures without worrying about rolls of film cluttering up your luggage. Storage media now have a capacity of up to a staggering 2 gigabytes. More important, however, is the ability to review immediately the image just taken and adjust the white balance, focus, metering and flash settings. This can save what might otherwise turn out to be a dive trip that produces unsatisfactory images.

The race for more megapixels has reached unprecedented heights, with even entry-level cameras such as the Nikon Coolpix range boasting 4–5 megapixels and high-end Nikon single lens range (SLR) digital cameras in excess of 10 megapixels. Having more megapixels, however, really only matters when printing images. It should also be noted at this point that megapixels do not compensate for the poor optical performance of lenses, which gives credence to the argument that brands such as Nikon continue to be at the forefront of quality and performance digital cameras.

General Considerations

General Diving Skills

For underwater photography, good diving skills, especially buoyancy control and feeling comfortable underwater, are essential. Apart from making the dive more enjoyable, these skills will have a huge impact on the type and quality of images that you take.

When encountering marine life, you are regarded as an alien visitor but not necessarily viewed as a threat. The underwater creatures know you are there and what you are doing long before you even see them. This is where having good diving skills pays off as the marine life is greatly attuned to body language. If you are uncomfortable underwater, bouncing up and down, kicking and thrashing around and noisily blowing bubbles, every creature within 20 metres will disappear into the ocean depths or into the nearest hole or crevice. If, however, you move slowly and breathe lightly to create fewer bubbles, marine life will often come over to investigate you. As you get close, the animals will react differently: some are afraid but rarely display aggressive behaviour; most often they do not seem to care. Keep in mind that the slowest fish in the sea is still faster than a scuba-laden human, so there is no point chasing anything as you will have nothing to show for your efforts except an empty tank. Good diving skills also impact the environment less, as coral and other marine life can be fragile and easily damaged.

Light and Colour Absorption and Surface Effects in Water

At a depth of 20 metres, virtually everything will appear to be in some sort of shade of blue and/or green. The same applies to a subject that is 20 metres away horizontally. (Although the human eye can compensate for this to a certain extent, film or digital imaging sensors have limitations.) This is because some light wavelengths are absorbed more efficiently by water than others. First, hues of red and orange disappear, followed by yellow, green and purple and, finally, blue. Loss of the colour red is dramatic and is already noticeable at a depth of 50 centimetres; at a depth of 5 metres almost 90 per cent will have disappeared. It should also be noted that brightness is also lessened, especially if the surface is rough.

Scatter Effect

Scatter, or the snow effect that bothers underwater photographers, is light bounced off visible particles. To minimise ambient scatter:

- shoot across the ambient light
- avoid ocean swell that stirs up sand and dust
- move cautiously and do not stir up the bottom
- move against the current, if possible
- dive in pairs: two divers create less disturbance.
- stay close to the subject.

Wide-Angle Photography

With wide-angle photography, the main subject is usually in the foreground. The subject matter can range from coral reef or gorgonian forest seascapes, shipwrecks and large animals like whale sharks to diver portraits and schools of fish. Such diverse shots are possible due to the use of a wide-angle lens, either with an amphibious camera like the Nikonos or a housed SLR. The all-time favourite must certainly be the Nikon 16mm fisheye lens that has an incredible 180 degrees picture angle and a short minimum focusing distance. Good results can also be achieved with either a 20mm or 28mm wide-angle lens.

Get Close, Shoot Up

This is the mantra for any underwater photographer. Get as close as you can, less than half a metre if feasible, to the subject matter. In addition, positioning yourself below the subject and shooting at an upward angle will put open water in the background, which is almost always better. Downward angles are more difficult to expose and tend to have a less aesthetic impact.

Ambient Light Exposure

This is the technique that is most often done incorrectly. If the ambient exposure is correct, many other factors will fall into place. The image will have a more 'natural' look and the use of fill-flash becomes much easier. If you are taking a silhouette of a subject with blue water in the background, the ambient exposure is about the only thing you need to get right. If you are photographing something like a shipwreck, it is not possible to light the whole object due to its size, so getting the correct ambient exposure is crucial.

So how do you get the right exposure? The solution comes from knowing how to meter the water in the background manually. Looking at the whole water column, decide which area represents the average and set the f-stop/shutter speed accordingly. Obviously, the extremes will not work: if metering off the sun, the image will be underexposed; likewise, metering dark rocks will result in overexposure. The sea can be various shades of blue and/or green depending on location, the amount of suspended solids, pollution, the condition of the sea and so on, but the principle is the same. Personally, I prefer to use center-weighted metering and bracket from there.

I would not recommend using the automatic mode function on your camera to select the correct exposure as it is not very reliable.

Using Strobes and Flashlights for Wide-Angle Shots

Flashlights or strobes are an integral part of underwater photography. For the most part, you will use them as fill-flash, restoring the colour and contrast that is inherently lost as you descend underwater. There are instances, however, when wide-angle shots require 100 per cent usage of strobes, such as at night or in the interior of a cave or shipwreck. Along with getting the right ambient light exposure, learning how to use strobes effectively is crucial.

Using strobes is not particularly hard but there are a number of choices to be made regarding equipment and approach. Simply put, you can either use the automatic through-the-lens (TTL) functions of the strobe of your housed camera or expose the strobe manually using guide numbers. Both techniques work but almost all pro and serious amateur photographers use the manual approach for wide-angle shots.

Through-The-Lens (TTL) Light Metering

Modern electronic cameras meter incoming light through the lens and control the shutter speed or aperture accordingly. These cameras can even measure the intensity of the strobe light during its fraction of a millisecond duration and, when sufficient, turn the strobe off before that millisecond has passed. They are also able to balance the accumulated strobe light to the ambient light.

Scatter from Strobe Light

Flashlight scatter is caused by brightly lit small objects that are close to the flashlight and the lens. It is a photographer's nightmare because it ruins the taken shot. As flashlight scatter is never visible when taking a photo, a number of techniques can be followed to reduce this effect:

- Move the strobe backwards so that it is behind the field of view covered by the lens. This can often be done easily by using the standard strobe arm.

- Move the strobe further out. You can do this yourself if you have a long arm or get your buddy to do it. By enlarging the distance, the lighting is no longer frontal but strongly sideways.

- Arrange a lighter background, particularly in the quarter of the image where the flashlight comes from. Even the sea can be used as the background as long as the ambient light is sufficiently allowed to expose the film.

- Use a wide flash reflector as this produces a softer kind of lighting.

- Use more available light. The amount of flashlight can be reduced by half, allowing for less strobe light and more ambient light. This is both easy to do and dramatic in result.

Macro Photography

Macro, or close-up, photography underwater shares many of the same concepts applicable for taking photos on dry land. The main difference is that ambient light is often not part of the equation. Generally, macro shots that include open water will appear with a black background. This is because there is insufficient ambient light to balance with the flash, unless a second strobe is used to lighten up the background and eliminate shadows.

Choosing the Right Equipment

Cameras

Most photographers will agree that you can take an outstanding image on land under the right conditions with a decent point-and-shoot or cheap SLR camera. Unfortunately, this is not the case underwater. Underwater photography is not more difficult but there are some specific optical problems that have to be overcome.

This is why some of the entry level brands give only marginal results at best. When choosing a camera, it all depends on what your expectations and goals are. If you just want to take some snapshots while snorkelling around Pulau Redang, these types of entry level brand cameras are fine. If, however, you expect sharp, publication-quality images, there really are no shortcuts. You do not have to sell all your belongings to own good underwater photographic equipment but cheap point-and-shoot cameras are going to be a disappointment. Here are some considerations to take into account when choosing a digital camera for underwater photography:

- If a camera has a high number of megapixels, it does not mean that the photographs you take will be better. It only means you can print larger images.

- The quality of the optics, i.e. lenses and ports, is crucial.

- The capacity of the memory device and write speed is important.

- The start-up and shutter lag delay should be short.

- The housing controls are comprehensive and correspond exactly to the camera controls. Underwater camera housings should be easy to use as making adjustments underwater while diving is a rather fiddly affair.

- The depth rating, i.e. the maximum depth of the housing, should correspond to your depth of diving.

Strobes and Flashes

Underwater flash units, often referred to as strobes, are essential, and not optional. The colour that is lost through the water column is a problem that will never go away. It is probably safe to assume that over 90 per cent of underwater images are taken using strobes. In theory, if you are less than 2 to 3 metres below the surface in clear water, it might not matter if you do not use a strobe. It will, however, most likely limit what photographic subjects are available. Even at shallow depths, a small amount of strobe will help with saturation and detail.

Entry level and prosumer digital cameras are equipped with an in-built flash unit. While this might appear sufficient, disappointment will soon set in, especially with wide-angle, openwater shots. As the flash unit is mounted either on top or slightly off-set, suspended solids in the water will reflect the light from the flash back into the lens and create backscatter or a snow effect. The way to overcome this problem is to use external strobes mounted on extensions of various lengths. These strobes will then provide more indirect light. An ideal manual strobe (or strobes) for a digital camera is one that has a variety of power settings, the easiest way to adjust artificial light to get the correct exposure and colour.

Lenses

For underwater photography, you have the choice of either wide-angle or macro lenses. The reason is simple: underwater, the biggest adversary is the water itself. Even crystal-clear tropical waters are not as clear as they seem. An even greater consideration is that the further light travels through the water, the more warm colours are absorbed. Therefore, the solution is to get as close as possible to the subject matter.

Wide-angle lenses such as the Nikon 16mm fisheye lens allow you to focus closely on large objects like reefs or whales but they still provide a view of the surrounding environment. Macro lenses, of course, work well since you are centimetres

away from the subject. Telephoto lenses, however, are useless underwater, as is any lens that forces you to work more than a few metres away from the subject.

Taking Care of Your Equipment

Rinse your underwater camera after every dive with fresh water or leave it to soak in a bucket of fresh water. Dry it carefully and inspect it for any damage.

O-ring maintenance is definitely the most important maintenance task. Housings, flashes, strobes and cables have O-ring seals to keep them dry and prevent flooding. Clean and slightly grease the O-ring with silicon. Then place the O-ring between your fingers and pull it through them to feel for imperfections and remove excess grease. Ensure the O-ring is properly seated before closing the housing. Although it is not necessary to grease the O-ring after every dive, always check for any sand or salt crystal deposit. If used regularly, put the O-ring into hot (but not boiling) water for about 5 minutes every few months. This will help to reduce the lengthening of the ring.

Some Tips on Digital Photography

Read the Instruction Manual, or at least some of it!

It seems that finding out how to open the battery compartment is the limit of many people's understanding of how a camera works. If you expect to use a digital camera without reading any of the manual, you will end up unhappy and will put away the camera in no time at all.

Apart from finding out how to do basic things like replacing batteries and memory cards and downloading images, the most

Cameras and Housings

Recommended cameras and housings that should cater for the requirements of beginners to professionals include:

SLR CAMERAS

Nikon F65: excellent entry level SLR
Nikon F80: the choice of the serious amateur
Nikon F100: standard equipment for every underwater photographer
Nikon F5: the best SLR camera that money can buy

Nikonos

Nikonos V: the all-time classic
Nikon RS: the only amphibious full-function SLR; costly and collectible

DIGITAL

Point-and-Shoot Cameras
Nikon Coolpix 2200, 3200, 4200, 5200
Prosumer Nikon 5700, 8700 (8 megapixels and flash socket)
Digital SLR (interchangeable lenses, flash)
Nikon D70 (6 megapixels)
Nikon D100 (6.1 megapixels)
Nikon D1X (5.7 megapixels)
Nikon D2H (4 megapixels)

BEST LENSES

Wide-angle: Nikon AF 16mm 2.8, Nikon AF 10.5mm 2.8 (DX), Nikon AF 20mm 2.8
Macro: Nikon AF 60mm 2.8, Nikon AF 105mm 2.8
Zoom: Nikon AF-S 12-24mm 2.8 (DX), Nikon AF-S 17-55mm 2.8 (DX)

FLASHES AND SUBSTROBES

Nikon SB 80DX & SB 800DX in housings
Ikelite 200 & DS 50

HOUSINGS

For more information on housings, check out the following websites:
Nikon (www.nikon.com)
SEACAM (www.seacam.com)
Ikelite (www.ikelite.com)
Sea & Sea (www.seaandsea.com)
Subal (www.subal.com)
Aquatica (www.aquatica.ca)
Amphibico (www.amphibico.com)

CAMERAS WITH MARINE PACKS

Nikon (for Coolpix 2200, 4200, 5200)
Canon (for Ixus A80, 550, s60, Ixus II)
Sony (for P100, P73 & 93, P10, T1)
Olympus (for 8800, 560, 750, 760, MJU 410)

important chapters to read are on White Balance, Flash, Image Quality, File Type and Size, Colour and Drive Mode.

The Auto White Balance Mode is forever improving. The latest models perform well outdoors and when the flash is used. However, if you are shooting underwater, with natural light or indoors, you need to get familiar with the camera's white balance options and learn when to use them.

The Flash function is important because it affects both the image and shooting speed. Normally, the camera will wait until the flash is ready to fire before it takes a picture. This can lead to a long delay and the loss of that 'award-winning' shot. If capturing a unique subject or moment, be

it a whale shark or your buddy getting harassed by a triggerfish, is more important than precise lighting or exposure, make sure the camera is set to a mode which will allow you to shoot when you want it to, not when it wants to.

Digital cameras are often sold with the image quality set to 'low'; probably to make the small memory cards that come with the camera seem useful. To obtain great images, take the time to set the right image quality. If you want good prints, pick the largest resolution jpeg with the least compression ratio. If you want to email your shots, an image size around 200 to 500 kilobytes will do nicely. Of course, you can always resize the image during post-processing and image editing.

Be Prepared

Commonly and erroneously, entry level and prosumer digital cameras are called point-and-shoot cameras. It would be more accurate to call them 'get ready, and then shoot' cameras. Taking any consumer digital camera and trying to snap a quick frame will produce garbage. Digital cameras need time to 'start up', acquire focus, check exposure and, if necessary, heat up the flash. Professionals have learned that even when using high-end cameras, it pays to be ready for the image you want ahead of time, i.e. have the camera 'hot' and the focus on the target before the action happens. Once your camera is ready to take the picture (i.e. the shutter release has been pressed half way and given time to adjust and turn on the 'ready' light), you will more likely to be able to capture the action.

Anticipate the action

Even when you have the camera ready, the subject perfectly positioned and composed, the shutter lag of the digital camera might still ruin the shot. You need to act quickly and even anticipate when the peak of the action will occur to give the camera time to take the picture when it does happen.

Hold steady

Always remember the shutter lag. You have to hold the camera steady until it has taken the picture. Many people forget that it takes a little time for the camera to take a picture and, instead of waiting, stab at the shutter release and start to move on before the camera has actually taken the picture. Many shots are ruined because of this.

The small size of consumer digital cameras often confuses photographers as well. Point-and-shoot models are actually much harder to hold still than heavier professional digital cameras or SLR cameras. It is also very tempting to wave these small cameras around. If you want to take good images, you have to work hard at mastering how to hold your small camera still. Practise holding the camera steady while looking at the liquid-crystal display (LCD). The old adage 'take a breath, hold it and slowly push the release' should work here as well.

Software

If you do decide to work with your images on your computer, you often do not need to use the software that comes with your camera. In fact, unless the software offers unique features, you may be able to avoid loading it at all. Most cameras are compatible with Windows XP and Mac OS X right out of the box. In other words, you can plug your camera into the computer and see your images immediately. Once you have the images on your computer, you can use whatever software you already have to process or print them.

Adobe Album 2.0 is a good choice for the casual photographer who uses Windows. Windows XP also has some built-in photo features including links to online photofinishers. If you want to experiment with editing your images, Photoshop Elements 2.0 is ideal. This package is bundled with many new computers and other digital devices. It is also inexpensive to buy. Post processing and image editing using software packages such as Adobe Photoshop or Adobe Elements can be used to rescue or enhance marginal images. Nikon's proprietary Nikon View & Capture is an excellent software suite for downloading and manipulating images. Capture Control enables the high-end digital models D100, D70, D1X and D2H to be operated and customised from a PC.

DIVE CENTRES IN MALAYSIA

Alu-Alu Divers
Teluk Dalam, Pulau Perhentian Besar
54200 Kuala Besut
Tel: (6) 019 376 8122
Fax: (60) 34 251 6757
Email: divemasters@alualudivers.com
Website: www.alualudivers.com

B & J Diving Centre
No. 46 Kampung Salang
Pulau Tioman
Pahang
Tel: (60) 9 419 5555
Fax: (60) 9 419 5554
Email: bjsalang@divetioman.com
Website: www.divetioman.com

Bali Hai Divers
Panuba Inn Resort, Panuba Bay
Kampung Panuba, Pulau Tioman
86807 Pahang
Tel: (6) 013 630 5008
Fax: (60) 6 336 9361
Email: enquiries@balihaidivers.net
Website: www.balihaidivers.net

Ballz Dive Centre
Lot 61, Jalan Maarof
Bangsar
59000 Kuala Lumpur
Tel: (60) 3 2284 8928
Fax: (60) 3 2284 8908
Email: dive@ballzaction.com
Website: www.ballzaction.com

Borneo Action Dive Centre
G19, Wisma Sabah
88000 Kota Kinabalu
Sabah
Tel/Fax: (60) 88 246 701
Email: info@borneoaction.com
Website: www.borneoaction.com

Borneo Divers & Sea Sports
9th Floor, Menara Jubili
53 Jalan Gaya
88000 Kota Kinabalu
Sabah
Tel: (60) 88 222 226
Fax: (60) 88 221 550
Email: information@borneodivers.info
Website: www.borneodivers.info

Bubu Long Beach Resort
Long Beach
Pulau Perhentian Kecil
Terengganu
Tel: (60) 9 697 8679
Fax: (60) 9 697 8679
Email: email@pulauperhentian.com.my

DC Scuba
45A & B, Persiaran Pegaga
Taman Bayu Perdana
41200 Klang
Tel: (60) 3 3324 9066
Fax: (60) 3 3324 3077
Email: info@dcscuba.com.my
Website: www.dcscuba.com.my

DiveAsia Tioman Island
Salang Village
Pulau Tioman
Pahang
Tel: (60) 9 419 5017
Email: diveasia@tm.net.my
Website: www.diveasia.com.my/

Eco-Divers
Tekek Beach, Pulau Tioman
86800 Pahang
Tel: (60) 9 419 1779 / (6) 013 602 2640
Email: divetioman@hotmail.com
Website: http://divemalaysia.i8.com

Elyzia Diving Club
#11 Retail Arcade
Sheraton Perdana Resort
Jalan Pantai, Dato Syed Omar
Langkawi
07000 Kedah
Tel: (60) 4 966 5182
Fax: (60) 4 966 4966

Flora Bay Divers
PADI 5 Star Gold Palm IDC Centre
Pulau Perhentian Besar
22300 Besut
Terengganu
Tel: (60) 9 6977 266 / (6) 013 943 6031
Email: info@florabaydivers.com
Website: www.florabaydivers.com

Laguna Redang Island Resort
Pasir Panjang
Pulau Redang
Tel: (60) 9 697 7888
Fax: (60) 9 697 8999
Email: enquiry@lagunaredang.com.my
Website: www.lagunaredang.com.my

Layang Layang Island Resort
A-0-3 Block A, Ground Floor
Megan Phileo Avenue II
12 Jalan Yap Kwan Seng
50450 Kuala Lumpur
Tel: (60) 3 2162 2877
Fax: (60) 3 2162 2980
Email: layang@pop.jaring.my
Website: www.layanglayang.com

Malayan Sub Aqua Club
73 Jalan Lai Tet Loke
50050 Kuala Lumpur
Email: aks5873@yahoo.com
Website: www.eperak.com/msac

Pan Borneo Tours & Travel
Location: Kota Kinabalu International Airport
Lot 2, Level 1, Domestic Arrival Hall
Kota Kinabalu International Airport
88740 Kota Kinabalu

Location: Sabah
Mailing address: P.O. Box 15447
88863 Kota Kinabalu, Sabah
Tel: (60) 88 221 221 / (60) 88 266 221
Fax: (60) 88 219 233
Email: info@panborneo.com
Website: www.panborneo.com

Planet Scuba
No 2, Jalan Telawi 5, Bangsar Baru
59100 Kuala Lumpur
Tel: (60) 3 2287 2822
Fax: (60) 3 2287 6922
Email: sales@planetscuba.com.my
Website: www.planetscuba.com.my

Pro Diver's World
Coral View Island Resort
Pulau Perhentian Besar
22300 Terengganu
Tel: (6) 019 363 3695
Fax: (60) 10 903 0200

Pulau Sipadan Resort & Tours
484 Bandar Sabindo
P.O. Box No. 61120
91021 Tawau
Sabah
Tel: (60) 89 765 200
Fax: (60) 89 763 575 / (60) 89 763 563
Email: info@sipadan-resort.com
Website: www.sipadan-resort.com

Redang Bay Resort Travel and Tours
139 Jalan Bandar
20100 Kuala Terengganu
Terengganu
Tel: (60) 9 620 3200
Fax: (60) 9 624 2048
Email: reservation@redangbay.com.my
Website: www.redangbay.com.my

Scuba Sarawak
Lot 1159, Miri Waterfront
Jalan Permaisuri
98000 Miri
Sarawak
Tel: (60) 85 428 225
Fax: (60) 85 428 227
Email: info@scubasa.com

Seaventures Tours & Travel
4th Floor, Room 422–424
Wisma Sabah
88300 Kota Kinabalu
Sabah
Tel: (60) 88 251 660 / (60) 88 251 669
Fax: (60) 88 251 667
Email: seavent@po.jaring.my
Website: www.seaventuresdives.com

Sipadan-Mabul Resort
2/F, Lot 8, Block B, Jalan Padas
Segama Complex
88000 Kota Kinabalu
Sabah
Tel: (60) 88 230 006
Fax: (60) 88 242 003
Email: mabul@po.jaring.my
Website: www.sipadan-mabul.com.my

Sipadan Water Village Resort
P.O. Box No. 62156
91031 Tawau, Sabah
Tel: (60) 89 752 996
Fax: (60) 89 752 997
Email: swv@sipadan-village.com.my
Website: www.sipadan-village.com.my

Spice Divers
Pulau Perhentian Kecil
22300 Besut
Tel: (6) 010 985 7329
Email: info@spicediver.com
Website: www.spicediver.com

Stingray Dive Centre
No. 2, MDB Long Beach
Pulau Perhentian Kecil
22300 Kuala Besut
Terengganu
Tel: (60) 9 697 7559 / (6) 019 946 0693
Fax: (60) 9 697 7559
Email: l-beach@tm.net.my
Website: www.geocities.com/stingraydivecentre

Sunrise Dive Centre
Kampung Juara
Pulau Tioman
86800 Pahang
Tel/Fax: (60) 9 419 3102
Email: info@sunrisedivecentre.com
Website: www.sunrisedivecentre.com

Tanjung Aru Tours & Travel
The Marina
Shangri-La Tanjung Aru Resort
WDT 14
89459 Kota Kinabalu
Sabah
Tel: (60) 88 222 210 / (60) 88 222 717
Fax: (60) 88 264 373
Email: tattsb@tm.net.my
Website: www.mattasabah.com/tanjungaru

Tioman Dive Centre
Kampung Tekek
86807 Pulau Tioman
Pahang
Tel/Fax: (60) 9 419 1228 / (6) 013 352 3389
Email: enquiries@tioman-dive-centre.com
Website: www.tioman-dive-centre.com/index.htm

Tropical Dives
No.1 Lobby Arcade, Park City Everly Hotel
Jalan Temenggong Datuk Oyong Lawai
98000 Miri
Sarawak
Tel: (60) 85 414 300
Fax: (60) 85 416 066
Email: info@tropical-dives.com
Website: www.tropical-dives.com

Turtle Bay Divers
Long Beach
Pulau Perhentian Kecil
Terengganu
Tel: (6) 019 333 6647 / (6) 019 910 6647
Tel (main office): (60) 3 7958 2527
Email: yaakub@tm.net.my / juarezp@tm.net.my
Website: www.turtlebaydivers.com/

GETTING TO MALAYSIA

The main international gateway to Malaysia is Kuala Lumpur, the country's capital city. Other key international gateways are Johor Bahru, Penang, Kuching and Kota Kinabalu.

By Air

Malaysia has five international airports: Kuala Lumpur International Airport (KLIA) (Tel: (60) 3 8777 8888; www.klia.com.my); Langkawi International Airport (Tel: (60) 4 955 1311); Penang International Airport (Tel: (60) 4 643 4411); Kota Kinabalu International Airport (Tel: (60) 88 238 555); and Kuching International Airport (Tel: (60) 82 454 242).

Malaysia Airlines, the country's national carrier, flies to over 100 international destinations as well as domestic destinations. (www.malaysiaairlines.com)

AirAsia, Malaysia's no frills, ticketless airline, offers low fares to domestic destinations and flights to Bangkok and Phuket in Thailand and Singapore. (www.airasia.com)

Other smaller aviation companies provide scheduled and chartered flights, such as Sabah Air (www.sabahair.com), Berjaya Air (www.berjaya-air.com) and Asia Tenggara Aviation Services (Tel: (60) 3 7783 0097).

By Land

PENINSULAR MALAYSIA

From Singapore: The Causeway links Singapore with Johor Bahru while the Second Link connects Singapore to Tanjung Kupang/Gelang Patah in Malaysia. Buses and taxis are readily available. Malaysia's national railway company Keretapi Tanah Melayu has daily trains to and from Singapore (www.ktmb.com.my).

From Thailand: The main border crossings from Thailand to Malaysia are Hat Yai–Padang Besar (by road or rail); Sadao–Bukit Kayu Hitam (by road); Betong–Keroh (by road); and Sungai Golok–Rantau Panjang (pedestrian crossing).

SARAWAK

From Brunei: Buses run from Bandar Seri Begawan in Brunei to Miri in Sarawak. Alternatively, taxis can be hired from Bangar in Brunei to Limbang or Lawas in Sarawak.

From Indonesia: Express buses operate from Pontianak in Kalimantan to Kuching in Sarawak.

For more information about Malaysia, go to the Tourism Malaysia website (www.tourismmalaysia.gov.my).